Collins

MATHS FRAMEWORKING

Complete success for Mathematics at KS3

YEAR 9

PUPIL BOOK 1

029

KEVIN EVANS **KEITH GORDON** **TREVOR SENIOR** **BRIAN SPEED**

Contents

CHAPTER 1 — Algebra 1 & 2

This chapter is going to show you

- how to generate and describe whole-number sequences
- how to see patterns in practical activities
- how to use term-to-term rules to create sequences
- how to express simple functions in symbols and to represent mappings algebraically
- how to generate points and plot graphs from linear equations

What you should already know

- How to use a flow diagram
- The basic rules of arithmetic
- How to plot coordinates and draw graphs

Sequences

Follow through the two flow diagrams in Examples 1.1 and 1.2, and write down the **sequence** of numbers each one generates.

Example 1.1

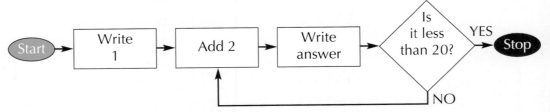

The flow diagram generates the sequence:

   1 3 5 7 9 11 13 15 17 19

These are the odd numbers less than 20.

The term-to-term rule is 'Add 2'.

Example 1.2

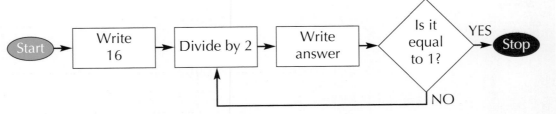

The flow diagram generates the sequence:

   16 8 4 2 1

This sequence of numbers can be described as halving to 1.

1. Work through each flow diagram below.

   i Write down each result.

   ii Write down a description of the numbers generated.

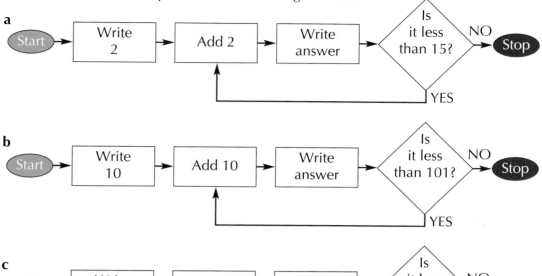

2. Work through each flow diagram below.

   Write down each result.

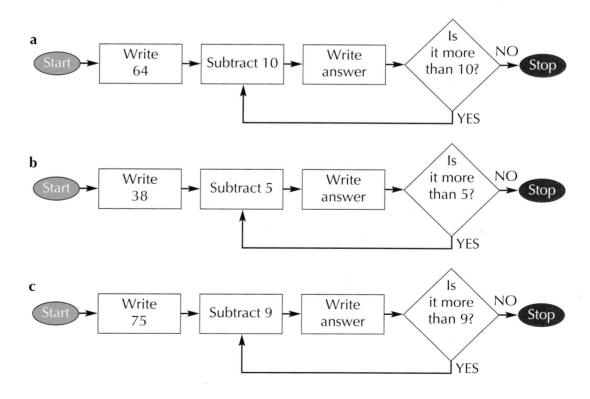

d

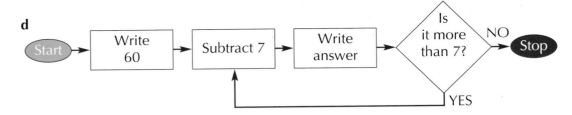

3 Work through each flow diagram below.

Write down each result.

a

b

c

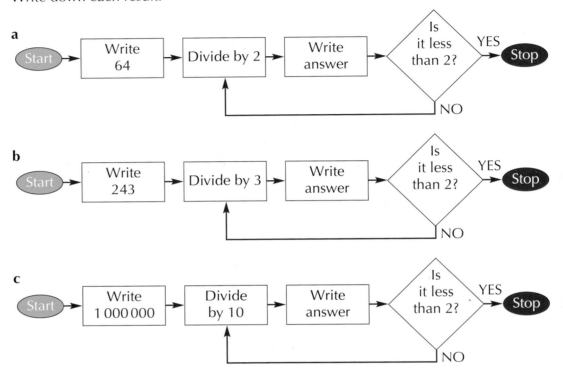

4 Draw a flow diagram for each of the following sequences.

    a   3, 6, 9, 15, 18, 21

    b   1, 5, 9, 13, 17, 21, 25

    c   3, 8, 13, 18, 23, 28, 33

    d   31, 29, 27, 25, 23, 21, 19

    e   66, 60, 54, 48, 42, 36, 30

    f   9, 20, 31, 42, 53, 64, 75

5 **i**   Write down the next two terms when each of the following sequences is continued.

    ii Describe each of the following sequences.

    a   31, 33, 35, 37, …

    b   35, 40, 45, 50, …

    c   28, 35, 42, 49, …

    d   32, 36, 40, 44, …

1   Work through this flow diagram. Write down the sequence which it generates.

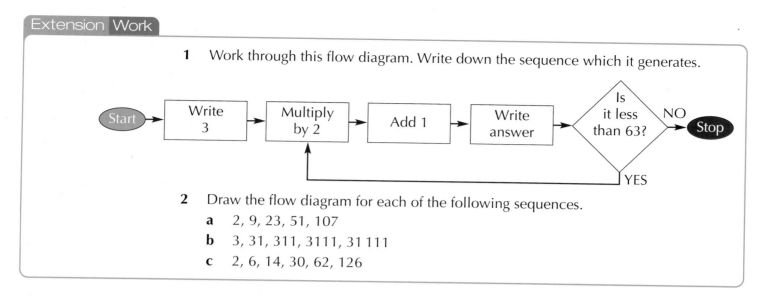

2   Draw the flow diagram for each of the following sequences.
   a   2, 9, 23, 51, 107
   b   3, 31, 311, 3111, 31 111
   c   2, 6, 14, 30, 62, 126

Sequences from patterns

Look at the pattern formed by these squares.

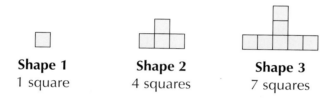

Shape 1   **Shape 2**   **Shape 3**
1 square   4 squares   7 squares

Can you see how many squares are needed to form the next two patterns?

The number of squares in shapes 1 to 3 gives the sequence 1, 4, 7, … . So, you will see that the sequence is generated by adding three more squares each time to the last pattern. That is, a square is added each time to each of the three arms of the pattern. Hence, shape 4 will have 7 + 3 = 10 squares and shape 5 will have 10 + 3 = 13 squares.

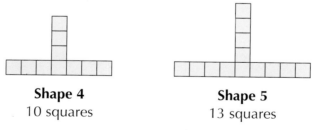

Shape 4   **Shape 5**
10 squares   13 squares

Look again at the pattern. Can you tell how many squares shape 10 has? It is too big to draw because that would take too long. So, can you find a rule which gives you the number of squares in any term of the sequence?

You will note that:
   Shape 2 has the first square + 1 × 3 = 4 squares
   Shape 3 has the first square + 2 × 3 = 7 squares
   Shape 4 has the first square + 3 × 3 = 10 squares

That is, the number of threes to add on is one less than the shape number. So, shape 10 has:

   First square + 9 × 3 = 28 squares

1 Look at this sequence of shapes.

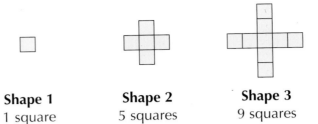

Shape 1
1 square

Shape 2
5 squares

Shape 3
9 squares

a Draw the next two shapes in the sequence, shape 4 and shape 5.
b Write down the number of squares in each of these shapes.
c Write down the term-to-term rule.
d Find how many squares there are in shape 10 without drawing it.

2 Look at this sequence of shapes.

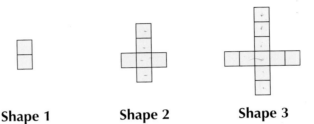

Shape 1

Shape 2

Shape 3

a Draw the next two shapes in the sequence, shape 4 and shape 5.
b Write down the number of squares in each of these shapes.
c Write down the term-to-term rule.
d Find how many squares there are in shape 10 without drawing it.

3 Look at this sequence of shapes.

Shape 1
2 lines

Shape 2
4 lines

Shape 3
6 lines

a Draw the next two shapes in the sequence, shape 4 and shape 5.
b Write down the number of lines in each of these shapes.
c Write down the term-to-term rule.
d Find how many lines there are in shape 11 without drawing it.

4 Look at this sequence of shapes.

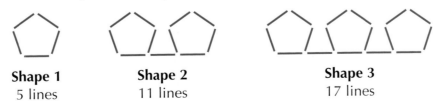

Shape 1
5 lines

Shape 2
11 lines

Shape 3
17 lines

a Draw the next two shapes in the sequence, shape 4 and shape 5.
b Write down the number of lines in each of these shapes.

c Write down the term-to-term rule.

d Find how many lines there are in shape 21 without drawing it.

5 Look at this sequence of shapes.

Shape 1	**Shape 2**	**Shape 3**
1 grey square	2 grey squares	3 grey squares
8 white squares	10 white squares	12 white squares

a Draw the next two shapes in this sequence, shape 4 and shape 5.

b Write down the number of grey squares in each of these shapes.

c Write down the number of white squares in each of these shapes.

d Without drawing the shapes:

   i Find how many grey squares there are in shape 10.

   ii Find how many white squares there are in shape 20.

   iii Find the total number of squares in shape 30.

6 Look at this sequence of shapes.

   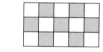   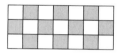

Shape 1   **Shape 2**   **Shape 3**

a Draw the next two shapes in this sequence, shape 4 and shape 5.

b Write down the number of grey squares in each of these shapes.

c Write down the number of white squares in each of these shapes.

d Without drawing the shapes:

   i Find how many grey squares there are in shape 10.

   ii Find how many white squares there are in shape 20.

   iii Find out the total number of squares in shape 30.

Look at this sequence of shapes.

Without drawing the shapes:

a Find how many grey triangles there are in shape 50.

b Find how many white triangles there are in shape 100.

c Find the total number of triangles in shape 500.

d Suppose you continue this pattern and in one shape you use 28 grey triangles. How many white ones would you need?

e Suppose you continue this pattern and in one shape you use 100 white triangles. How many grey ones would you need?

f What is the number of the shape which has 998 triangles?

The nth term of a sequence

The position of a term in a sequence can sometimes be used to find its value. The idea is to find a general term, called the **nth term**, from which the value of any term can be found. Look at Examples 1.3 and 1.4 to see how this works.

Example 1.3 ▷ Find the nth term for the sequence given below.

Position number, n 1 2 3 4 5

Value of term   5 6 7 8 9

Each term can be found by adding 4 to its position number, n. So, the nth term is given by $n + 4$.

Example 1.4 ▷ Write down the first five terms of a sequence where the nth term is given by $2n + 3$.

To find each term, give the position number, n, the value 1 to 5, in order, as shown below.

$$n \longrightarrow 2n + 3$$

or $n \longrightarrow \boxed{\times 2} \longrightarrow \boxed{+3} \longrightarrow$ Value of term

The 1st term is:	1	$\longrightarrow$ 2 $\longrightarrow$	5
The 2nd term is:	2	$\longrightarrow$ 4 $\longrightarrow$	7
The 3rd term is:	3	$\longrightarrow$ 6 $\longrightarrow$	9
The 4th term is:	4	$\longrightarrow$ 8 $\longrightarrow$	11
The 5th term is:	5	$\longrightarrow$ 10 $\longrightarrow$	13

Hence, the sequence is 5, 7, 9, 11, 13, ...

When you are given a rule like this, you can use it to find a term well into the sequence. For example, the 50th term in the above sequence is found by putting $n = 50$ into $n \longrightarrow 2n + 3$, which gives:

$n \longrightarrow \boxed{\times 2} \longrightarrow \boxed{+3} \longrightarrow$ Value of term

50    $\longrightarrow$ 100 $\longrightarrow$ 103

Exercise 1C

1 The nth term of a sequence is given by $n \longrightarrow 5n + 2$

   a   Find the first five terms of the sequence.

   b   Find the 20th term of the sequence.

   c   Find the 50th term of the sequence.

2 The nth term of a sequence is given by $n \longrightarrow 7n - 1$

   a   Find the first five terms of the sequence.

   b   Find the 10th term of the sequence.

   c   Find the 100th term of the sequence.

3 The nth term of a sequence is given by $n \longrightarrow 4n + 9$

    a   Find the first five terms of the sequence.

    b   Find the 30th term of the sequence.

    c   Find the 150th term of the sequence.

4 The nth term of a sequence is given by $n \longrightarrow 100 + 2n$

    a   Find the first five terms of the sequence.

    b   Find the 10th term of the sequence.

    c   Find the 50th term of the sequence.

5 The nth term of a sequence is given by $n \longrightarrow 100 - 2n$

    a   Find the first five terms of the sequence.

    b   Find the 20th term of the sequence.

    c   Find the 50th term of the sequence.

6 Look at the pattern below.

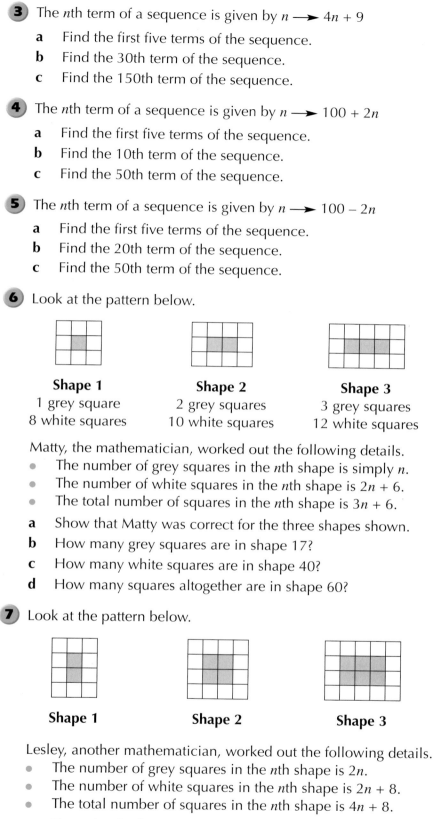

Shape 1	**Shape 2**	**Shape 3**
1 grey square	2 grey squares	3 grey squares
8 white squares	10 white squares	12 white squares

Matty, the mathematician, worked out the following details.
- The number of grey squares in the nth shape is simply n.
- The number of white squares in the nth shape is $2n + 6$.
- The total number of squares in the nth shape is $3n + 6$.

    a   Show that Matty was correct for the three shapes shown.

    b   How many grey squares are in shape 17?

    c   How many white squares are in shape 40?

    d   How many squares altogether are in shape 60?

7 Look at the pattern below.

Shape 1	**Shape 2**	**Shape 3**

Lesley, another mathematician, worked out the following details.
- The number of grey squares in the nth shape is $2n$.
- The number of white squares in the nth shape is $2n + 8$.
- The total number of squares in the nth shape is $4n + 8$.

    a   Show that Lesley was correct for the three shapes shown.

    b   How many grey squares are in shape 13?

    c   How many white squares are in shape 20?

    d   How many squares altogether are in shape 100?

1   Create a series of shapes, whose *n*th shape has 4*n* + 1 squares.

2   Create a series of shapes, whose *n*th shape has 3*n* + 1 squares.

3   Create a series of shapes, whose *n*th shape has **a**   *n* grey squares and
    b   4*n* white squares.

4   Create a series of shapes, whose *n*th shape has **a**   2*n* grey squares and
    b   3*n* white squares.

5   Create a series of shapes, whose *n*th shape has **a**   3*n* grey squares and
    b   6*n* white squares.

Combined functions and mappings

A **function** is a rule which changes one number, called the **input**, to another number, called the **output**. It involves any one or more of the following operations: addition, subtraction, multiplication, division.

A function can also be defined as a mapping which has *only one* output number for every input. Example 1.5 shows how this works.

Example 1.5   Draw a mapping diagram to illustrate the following.

Input ⟶ | Multiply by 2 | ⟶ | Add 3 | ⟶ Output

Start with any set of numbers as the input. Each input maps with the function to the output. So, for the function

Input ⟶ | Multiply by 2 | ⟶ | Add 3 | ⟶ Output

0	⟶	0	⟶	3
1	⟶	2	⟶	5
2	⟶	4	⟶	7
3	⟶	6	⟶	9

The mapping | Multiply by 2 | can be written using algebra as $x \longrightarrow 2x$.

The mapping | Add 3 | can be written using algebra as $x \longrightarrow x + 3$.

Hence, the combined mapping | Multiply by 2 | ⟶ | Add 3 | can be represented by $x \longrightarrow 2x + 3$.

The function $x \longrightarrow 2x + 3$ has this mapping diagram:

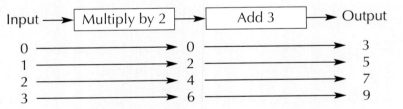

x	⟶	$2x + 3$
0	⟶	3
1	⟶	5
2	⟶	7
3	⟶	9

From this, you can see that a function may be thought of as a machine which processes numbers. Take as an example $x \longrightarrow 2x + 3$:

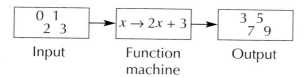

Input   Function   Output
       machine

1 Copy and complete each of the following mapping diagrams for the functions shown.

a

| Multiply by 3 | Add 5 | | Combined as |

Input   Output $x \longrightarrow 3x + 5$

0	→	☐	→	·	0 → ☐
1	→	3	→	8	1 → 8
2	→	☐	→	☐	2 → ☐
3	→	☐	→	☐	3 → ☐

b

| Multiply by 5 | Add 4 | | Combined as |

Input   Output $x \longrightarrow 5x + 4$

0	→	☐	→	☐	0 → ☐
1	→	5	→	9	1 → 9
2	→	☐	→	☐	2 → ☐
3	→	☐	→	☐	3 → ☐

c

| Multiply by 4 | Add 7 | | Combined as |

Input   Output $x \longrightarrow 4x + 7$

0	→	☐	→	☐	0 → ☐
1	→	4	→	11	1 → 11
2	→	☐	→	☐	2 → ☐
3	→	☐	→	☐	3 → ☐

2 Copy and complete each of the following mapping diagrams for the functions shown.

a

| Add 5 | Multiply by 3 | | Combined as |

Input   Output $x \longrightarrow 3(x + 5)$

0	→	☐	→	☐	0 → ☐
1	→	6	→	18	1 → 18
2	→	☐	→	☐	2 → ☐
3	→	☐	→	☐	3 → ☐

b

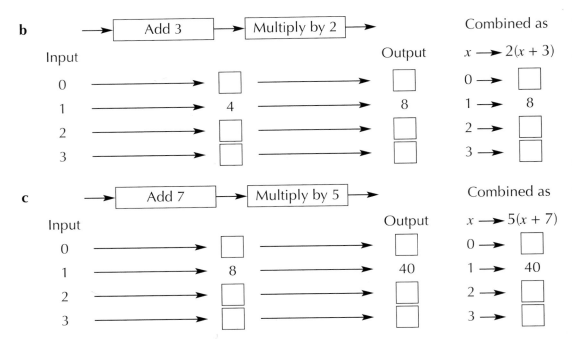

Add 3 → Multiply by 2 → Combined as

Input			Output	$x \longrightarrow 2(x+3)$
0				0 →
1	4		8	1 → 8
2				2 →
3				3 →

c

Add 7 → Multiply by 5 → Combined as

Input			Output	$x \longrightarrow 5(x+7)$
0				0 →
1	8		40	1 → 40
2				2 →
3				3 →

3 Copy and complete the mapping diagram for each of the following combined functions.

a $x \longrightarrow 4x + 3$

0 →
1 →
2 →
3 → 15

b $x \longrightarrow 2x + 9$

0 →
1 →
2 →
3 →

c $x \longrightarrow 2(x + 8)$

0 →
1 →
2 →
3 →

4 Draw mapping diagrams to illustrate each of the following functions.

a $x \longrightarrow 5x + 3$ **b** $x \longrightarrow 4x + 1$ **c** $x \longrightarrow 3(x + 4)$

5 For each function, draw a mapping diagram using algebra.

a 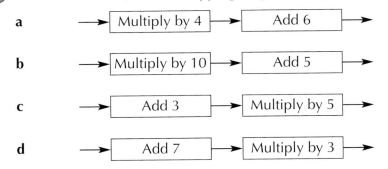 → Multiply by 4 → Add 6 →

b → Multiply by 10 → Add 5 →

c → Add 3 → Multiply by 5 →

d → Add 7 → Multiply by 3 →

6 Write down what should be in each box in each of the following mapping diagrams.

a

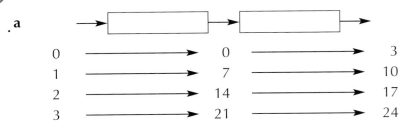

0	→	0	→	3
1	→	7	→	10
2	→	14	→	17
3	→	21	→	24

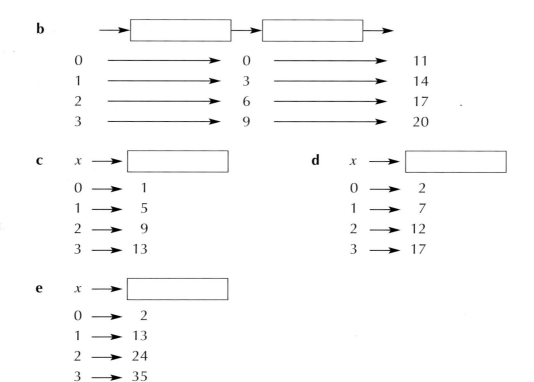

b

0 →	0 → 11
1 →	3 → 14
2 →	6 → 17
3 →	9 → 20

c $x →$ [ ]

0 → 1
1 → 5
2 → 9
3 → 13

d $x →$ [ ]

0 → 2
1 → 7
2 → 12
3 → 17

e $x →$ [ ]

0 → 2
1 → 13
2 → 24
3 → 35

Extension Work

Create mapping diagrams to illustrate each of the following.

a $x → 3x - 1$ **b** $x → 4x - 5$ **c** $x → 5x - 8$

d $x → 10 - x$ **e** $x → 10 - 2x$ **f** $x → 10 - 3x$

Graphs of functions

There are different ways to write functions. For example, the function

$$x → 3x + 1$$

can also be written as

$$y = 3x + 1$$

with the inputs as x and the outputs as y.

This alternative way of writing functions simplifies the drawing of graphs. Every function has its own graph which is produced by finding ordered pairs of numbers, or coordinates, from the function, and plotting them.

Note The graph of any linear function is a straight line.

Example 1.6 ⟩   Draw a graph of the function $y = 3x + 1$.

First, make a table of easy values for the x-coordinates. Then calculate the corresponding values of y, using $y = 3x + 1$. These y-coordinates are also put in the table.

x	−1	0	1	2	3
$y = 3x + 1$	−2	1	4	7	10

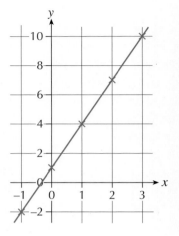

Then, either construct a grid or use suitably graduated graph paper, marking the x-axis from −1 to 3 and the y-axis from −2 to 10. Next, plot the coordinates and join them to give a straight line graph.

Note that this graph passes through countless other coordinates, all of which obey the same rule of the function: that is, $y = 3x + 1$. You can choose any point on the line which has not been plotted to show that this is true.

Exercise 1E

1 a   Copy and complete the table below for the function $y = x + 2$.

x	−1	0	1	2	3
$y = x + 2$	1	2			

b   Draw a grid with its x-axis from −1 to 3 and y-axis from −1 to 5.

c   Use the table to construct, on the grid, the graph of the function $y = x + 2$.

2 a   Copy and complete the table below for the function $y = 2x + 3$.

x	−1	0	1	2	3
$y = 2x + 3$	1	3			

b   Draw a grid with its x-axis from −1 to 3 and y-axis from −1 to 9.

c   Use the table to construct, on the grid, the graph of the function $y = 2x + 3$.

3 a   Copy and complete the table below for the function $y = 4x + 2$.

x	−1	0	1	2	3
$y = 4x + 2$	−2	2			

b   Draw a grid with its x-axis from −1 to 3 and y-axis from −2 to 14.

c   Use the table to construct, on the grid, the graph of the function $y = 4x + 2$.

4 a   Copy and complete the table below for the function $y = 5x + 1$.

x	−1	0	1	2	3
$y = 5x + 1$	−4	1			

b   Draw a grid with its x-axis from −1 to 3 and y-axis from −4 to 16.

c   Use the table to construct, on the grid, the graph of the function $y = 5x + 1$.

5 a Copy and complete the table below for the functions shown.

x	−1	0	1	2	3
$y = 2x + 1$	−1				7
$y = 2x + 2$	0			6	
$y = 2x + 3$	1	3	5		
$y = 2x$	−2	0	2		

b Draw a grid with its x-axis from −1 to 3 and y-axis from −2 to 11.

c Draw the graph for each function in the table above.

d What two properties do you notice about each line?

e Use the properties you have noticed to draw the graph of each of the following functions.

    i $y = 2x + 4$ **ii** $y = 2x + 5$

6 a Copy and complete the table below for the functions shown.

x	−1	0	1	2	3
$y = 3x + 1$					10
$y = 3x + 2$	−1			8	
$y = 3x + 3$		3			
$y = 3x + 4$			7		

b Draw a grid with its x-axis from −1 to 3 and y-axis from −2 to 13.

c Draw the graph for each function in the table above.

d What two properties do you notice about each line?

e Use the properties you have noticed to draw the graph of each of the functions.

    i $y = 3x + 5$ **ii** $y = 3x + 6$ **iii** $y = 3x$

Extension Work

Draw the graph of $y = 4x + 1$ and of $y = 4x + 5$.

Now draw, without any further calculations, the graph of $y = 4x + 3$ and of $y = 4x + 7$.

What you need to know for level 4

- Be able to work through a simple flow diagram
- Be able to draw simple shapes to follow a pattern
- How to draw mapping diagrams
- How to use a simple algebraic expression to determine a sequence

What you need to know for level 5

- Be able to find the next few terms of a given sequence
- How to make a prediction from a given pattern
- How to draw graphs from simple functions

National Curriculum SATs questions

LEVEL 4

1 *2000 Paper 1*

54 is put into each number machine. Write down the numbers that come out.

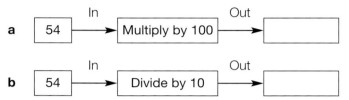

2 *1998 Paper 2*

Owen has some tiles like these:

He uses the tiles to make a series of patterns.

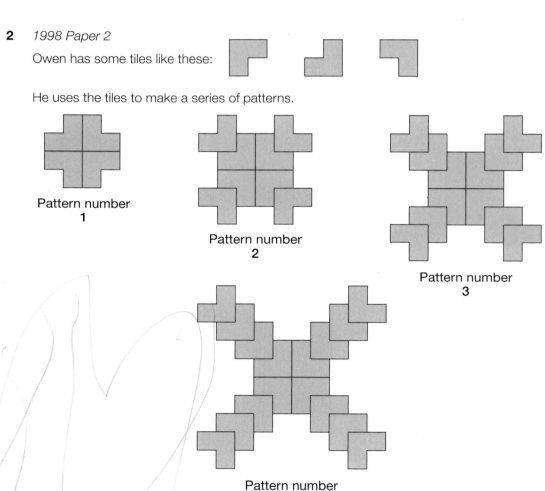

Pattern number
1

Pattern number
2

Pattern number
3

Pattern number
4

a Each new pattern has more tiles than the one before. The number of tiles goes up by the same amount each time.

How many more tiles does Owen add each time he makes a new pattern?

b How many tiles will Owen need altogether to make pattern number 6?

c How many tiles will Owen need altogether to make pattern number 9?

d Owen uses 40 tiles to make a pattern. What is the number of the pattern he makes?

LEVEL 5

3 *1999 Paper 2*

Jeff makes a sequence of patterns with black and grey tiles.

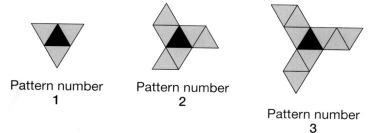

Pattern number
1

Pattern number
2

Pattern number
3

The rule for finding the number of tiles in pattern number N in Jeff's sequence is:

Number of tiles = $1 + 3N$

a The 1 in this rule represents the black tile. What does the $3N$ represent?

b Jeff makes pattern number 12 in his sequence. How many black tiles and how many grey tiles does he use?

c Jeff uses 61 tiles altogether to make a pattern in his sequence. What is the number of the pattern he makes?

d Barbara makes a sequence of patterns with hexagonal tiles.

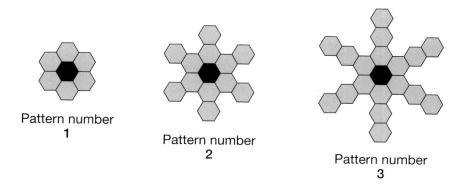

Pattern number
1

Pattern number
2

Pattern number
3

Each pattern in Barbara's sequence has 1 black tile in the middle. Each new pattern has 6 more grey tiles than the pattern before.

Write the rule for finding the number of tiles in pattern number N in Barbara's sequence.

Number of tiles = ... + ...

e Gwenno uses some tiles to make a different sequence of patterns. The rule for finding the number of tiles in pattern number N in Gwenno's sequence is

Number of tiles = $1 + 4N$

Draw what you think the first three patterns in Gwenno's sequence could be.

4 *2000 Paper 2*

You can make 'huts' with matches.

| 1 hut needs 5 matches | 2 huts need 9 matches | 3 huts need 13 matches |

A rule to find how many matches you need is:

$$m = 4h + 1$$

m stands for the number of matches, h stands for the number of huts.

a   Use the rule to find how many matches you need to make 8 huts. Show your working.

b   I use 81 matches to make some huts. How many huts do I make? Show your working.

c   Andy makes different 'huts' with matches.

| 1 hut needs 6 matches | 2 huts need 11 matches | 3 huts need 16 matches |

Write down the rule below that shows how many matches you need.

Remember: m stands for the number of matches; h stands for the number of huts.

$m = h + 5$ $m = 4h + 2$ $m = 4h + 3$

$m = 5h + 1$ $m = 5h + 2$ $m = h + 13$

This chapter is going to show you

- how to order decimals
- how to calculate with fractions, percentages and ratio
- how to round numbers to two decimal places

What you should already know

- How to order integers
- Some simple equivalent fractions, decimals and percentages
- How to find simple equivalent fractions

Ordering decimals

Name	Leroy	Myrtle	Jack	Baby Jane	Alf	Doris
Age	37.4	21	$32\frac{1}{2}$	9 months	57	68 yrs 3 mths
Height	170 cm	1.54 m	189 cm	0.55 m	102 cm	1.80 m
Weight	75 kg	50.3 kg	68 kg	7.5 kg	85 kg	76 kg 300 g

Look at the people in the picture. How would you put them in order?

When you compare the size of numbers, you have to consider the **place value** of each digit. This is the value given to a digit because of the position the digit has in the number relative to the units place.

It helps if you fill in the numbers in a table like the one shown on the right.

The decimal point separates the whole-number part of the number from the decimal-fraction part.

Example 2.1 explains how the table works.

Thousands	Hundreds	Tens	Units	Tenths	Hundredths	Thousandths
			5	6	6	0
			5	0	6	0
			5	6	0	7

Example 2.1 ▷ Put the numbers 5.66, 5.06 and 5.607 in order, from smallest to largest.

The numbers are shown in the table. Zeros have been added to make up the missing decimal places in the last column.

Working across the table from the left, you can see that all of the numbers have the same units digit. Two of them have the same tenths digit, and two have the same hundredths digit. But only one has a digit in the thousandths.

Note that 5.660 is bigger than 5.060 because it has more tenths. It is also bigger than 5.607 because it has more hundredths. And 5.607 is bigger than 5.060 because it has more tenths.

So, the order is:

5.06, 5.607, 5.66

Example 2.2 ▷ Put the correct sign, > or <, between each of these pairs of numbers:

a 3.02 and 3.013   **b** 0.05 and 0.054.

a Both numbers have the same units and tenths digits, but the hundredths digit is bigger in the first number. So, the answer is 3.02 > 3.013.

b Both numbers have the same units, tenths and hundredths digits. But the second number has the bigger thousandths digit, as the first number has a zero in the thousandths. So, the answer is 0.05 < 0.054.

Exercise 2A

1 a Copy the table on page 19 (but not the numbers). Write the following numbers in the table, placing each digit in the appropriate column.

5.68, 56, 5.068, 5.6, 0.056, 0.6, 5.06

b Use your answer to part **a** to write the numbers in order from smallest to largest.

2 Write each of these sets of numbers in order from smallest to largest.

a 0.63, 0.063, 0.7, 0.609, 0.6

b 1.607, 1.7, 1.809, 1.808, 1.8

c 23, 2.3, 0.23, 1.23, 0.023

3 Put the correct sign, > or <, between each of these pairs of numbers.

a 0.435   0.445   **b** 0.73   0.703   **c** 5.23   5.204

d 6.36 km   6.336 km   **e** 0.567 kg   0.6 kg   **f** £0.04   6p

4 Put the following amounts of money in order, smallest first.

a 108p   £0.80   78p   £0.65   £0.09

b £0.90   89p   £9   10p   £0.68

5 Put these times in order: 1 hour 10 minutes, 25 minutes, 1.25 hours, 0.5 hours.

6 One metre is 100 centimetres. Change all the lengths below to metres and then put them in order from smallest to largest.

4.45 m, 349 cm, 20 cm, 3.5 m, 0.24 m

7 One kilogram is 1000 grams. Change all the weights below to kilograms and then put them in order from smallest to largest.

37 g, 1.370 kg, 37 kg, 0.4 kg, 0.036 kg

8 Write each of the following statements in words.

a $3.1 < 3.14 < 3.142$

b £0.07 < 32p < £0.56

Adding and subtracting fractions

This section will give you more practice with adding and subtracting fractions.

Example 2.3

Work out:

a $\frac{3}{4} + 1\frac{1}{8}$ **b** $1\frac{7}{8} - \frac{3}{4}$

Previously, we used a fraction chart or line to do these. An eighths fraction line is drawn below.

a Start at 0 and count on $\frac{3}{4}$, then 1 and then $\frac{1}{8}$ to give $\frac{3}{4} + 1\frac{1}{8} = 1\frac{7}{8}$.

b Start at $1\frac{7}{8}$ and count back $\frac{3}{4}$ to give $1\frac{7}{8} - \frac{3}{4} = 1\frac{1}{8}$.

When a fraction line is not used and the denominators of the fractions are not the same, they must be made the same before the numerators are added or subtracted. To do this, we need to find the **Lowest Common Multiple (LCM)** of the denominators.

Example 2.4 ▷

Work out:

a $\frac{1}{3} + \frac{1}{4}$ b $\frac{5}{9} - \frac{1}{6}$

a   The LCM of 3 and 4 is 12, so the two fractions need to be written as twelfths:

$$\frac{1}{3} + \frac{1}{4} = \frac{4}{12} + \frac{3}{12} = \frac{7}{12}$$

b   The LCM of 9 and 6 is 18, so the two fractions need to be written as eighteenths:

$$\frac{5}{9} - \frac{1}{6} = \frac{10}{18} - \frac{3}{18} = \frac{7}{18}$$

Exercise 2B

1   Work out each of the following (the fraction line on page 21 may help).

   a $\frac{3}{8} + \frac{1}{2}$ b $1\frac{3}{8} + \frac{1}{8}$ c $1\frac{1}{8} + 2\frac{5}{8}$ d $1\frac{1}{2} + 1\frac{3}{4} + 1\frac{5}{8}$

   e $\frac{7}{8} - \frac{1}{2}$ f $1\frac{3}{8} - \frac{7}{8}$ g $2\frac{1}{8} - 1\frac{3}{8}$ h $1\frac{1}{4} + 1\frac{1}{2} - 1\frac{3}{8}$

2   Work out each of the following. Cancel down the answers to their lowest terms and convert improper (top-heavy) fractions to mixed numbers.

   a $\frac{1}{7} + \frac{1}{7}$ b $\frac{3}{4} + \frac{3}{4}$ c $\frac{2}{5} + \frac{2}{5}$ d $\frac{1}{3} + \frac{2}{3} + \frac{2}{3}$

   e $\frac{13}{15} - \frac{4}{15}$ f $\frac{8}{9} - \frac{5}{9}$ g $\frac{10}{12} - \frac{4}{12}$ h $\frac{3}{10} + \frac{9}{10} - \frac{5}{10}$

3   Firstly, convert the following fractions to equivalent fractions with a common denominator, and then work out the answer, cancelling down or writing as a mixed number as appropriate.

   a $\frac{1}{5} + \frac{1}{4}$ b $\frac{1}{8} + \frac{1}{2}$ c $\frac{3}{4} + \frac{1}{5}$ d $\frac{1}{6} + \frac{2}{9}$

   e $\frac{5}{7} + \frac{1}{2}$ f $\frac{3}{8} + \frac{2}{5}$ g $\frac{5}{6} + \frac{1}{4}$ h $\frac{2}{5} + \frac{1}{10} + \frac{1}{2}$

   i $\frac{1}{4} - \frac{1}{5}$ j $\frac{5}{8} - \frac{1}{3}$ k $\frac{3}{4} - \frac{1}{5}$ l $\frac{5}{6} - \frac{2}{3}$

   m $\frac{4}{5} - \frac{7}{10}$ n $\frac{3}{8} - \frac{1}{5}$ o $\frac{3}{8} - \frac{1}{4}$ p $\frac{2}{5} + \frac{1}{10} - \frac{1}{2}$

4   A magazine has $\frac{1}{4}$ of its pages for advertising, $\frac{1}{12}$ for letters and the rest for articles.

   a   What fraction of the pages is for articles?

   b   If the magazine has 150 pages, how many are used for articles?

5   A survey of students showed that $\frac{1}{5}$ of them walked to school, $\frac{1}{3}$ came by bus and the rest came by car.

   a   What fraction came by car?

   b   If there were 1200 students in the school, how many came by car?

6   A farmer plants $\frac{2}{7}$ of his land with wheat and $\frac{5}{8}$ with maize; the rest is used for cattle.

   a   What fraction of the land is used to grow crops?

   b   What fraction is used for cattle?

Consider the series $\frac{1}{2} + \frac{1}{4} + \frac{1}{8} + \frac{1}{16} + \frac{1}{32} + \frac{1}{64} + \frac{1}{128} \dots$. If we write down the first term, then add the first two terms, then add the first three terms, we obtain the sequence $\frac{1}{2}, \frac{3}{4}, \frac{7}{8}, \dots$.

a Continue this sequence for another four terms.

b What total will the sequence reach if it continues for an infinite number of terms?

c Repeat with the series $\frac{1}{3} + \frac{1}{9} + \frac{1}{27} + \frac{1}{81} + \frac{1}{243} + \frac{1}{729} + \frac{1}{2187} \dots$.

Multiplying and dividing fractions

So far, you have seen how to add and to subtract fractions. In this section, you will multiply and divide fractions. Surprisingly, this is easier.

Example 2.5 Jan's watering can is $\frac{3}{5}$ full. She waters her roses and uses half of this water. How full is her watering can now?

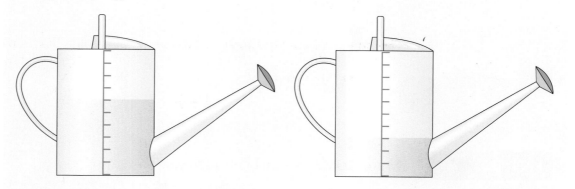

As you can see from the diagram, Jan's watering can is $\frac{3}{10}$ full after she has watered the roses. How can you calculate this result?

One half of $\frac{3}{5}$ is written as:

$$\frac{1}{2} \times \frac{3}{5} = \frac{1 \times 3}{2 \times 5} = \frac{3}{10}$$

This shows that when a fraction is multiplied by another fraction, the new numerator is found by multiplying together the two original numerators, and the new denominator by multiplying together the two original denominators.

Example 2.6 ▶   Work out $\frac{3}{4} \times \frac{2}{9}$

Following Example 2.5, you can calculate mentally that the answer is $\frac{6}{36}$, which can be cancelled to $\frac{1}{6}$. However, this is an example of where it is easier to cancel before you complete the multiplication.

When numerators and denominators have factors in common, you can cancel them. In this example, 3 and 9 will cancel, as do 2 and 4. The calculation is therefore given like this:

$$\frac{\cancel{3}^{1}}{\cancel{4}_{2}} \times \frac{\cancel{2}^{1}}{\cancel{9}_{3}} = \frac{1}{6}$$

The remaining numbers are multiplied together to give the new numerator and the new denominator. When the fractions are cancelled properly, the final answer will not cancel.

Example 2.7 ▶   Work out each of these.

    a $\frac{3}{5} \div \frac{1}{4}$ **b** $\frac{15}{24} \div \frac{9}{16}$

    a   When you are dividing by a fraction, always use the following rule:

         Turn the dividing fraction upside down and multiply by it.

       So, you have:

$$\frac{3}{5} \div \frac{1}{4} = \frac{3}{5} \times \frac{4}{1} = \frac{3 \times 4}{5 \times 1} = \frac{12}{5} = 2\frac{2}{5}$$

    b   When possible, cancel during the multiplication.

$$\frac{15}{24} \div \frac{9}{16} = \frac{\cancel{15}^{5}}{\cancel{24}_{3}} \times \frac{\cancel{16}^{2}}{\cancel{9}_{3}} = \frac{5 \times 2}{3 \times 3} = \frac{10}{9} = 1\frac{1}{9}$$

Exercise 2C

1   Cancel down each of the following fractions.

    a $\frac{3}{9}$ **b** $\frac{6}{18}$ **c** $\frac{4}{10}$ **d** $\frac{6}{15}$

    e $\frac{10}{25}$ **f** $\frac{7}{14}$ **g** $\frac{9}{12}$ **h** $\frac{9}{15}$

    i $\frac{12}{20}$ **j** $\frac{18}{30}$

2   Work out each of the following. Cancel before multiplying when possible.

    a $\frac{1}{3} \times \frac{2}{5}$ **b** $\frac{3}{4} \times \frac{3}{4}$ **c** $\frac{2}{7} \times \frac{5}{8}$ **d** $\frac{3}{8} \times \frac{4}{9}$

    e $\frac{5}{8} \times \frac{12}{25}$ **f** $\frac{5}{6} \times \frac{3}{5}$ **g** $\frac{1}{2} \times \frac{6}{11}$ **h** $\frac{1}{4} \times \frac{8}{15}$

    i $\frac{3}{4} \times \frac{8}{9}$ **j** $\frac{3}{5} \times \frac{15}{22} \times \frac{11}{18}$

3   Work out each of the following. Cancel at the multiplication stage when possible.

    a $\frac{1}{2} \div \frac{1}{8}$ **b** $\frac{2}{3} \div \frac{3}{5}$ **c** $\frac{5}{6} \div \frac{2}{3}$ **d** $\frac{1}{3} \div \frac{6}{7}$

    e $\frac{4}{5} \div \frac{3}{10}$ **f** $\frac{5}{8} \div \frac{15}{16}$ **g** $\frac{2}{7} \div \frac{7}{8}$ **h** $\frac{3}{4} \div \frac{9}{13}$

    i $\frac{1}{2} \div \frac{3}{5}$ **j** $\frac{1}{4} \div \frac{3}{8}$

4 A rectangle has sides of $\frac{3}{7}$ cm and $\frac{14}{27}$ cm. Calculate its area.

5 A rectangle has sides of $\frac{3}{4}$ cm and $\frac{8}{9}$ cm. Calculate its area.

Extension Work

The rules of BODMAS apply when working with fractions.
Work out each of these.

a $\left(\frac{3}{4} \div \frac{9}{16} \times \frac{3}{4}\right)$ **b** $\left(\frac{3}{8} \div \frac{1}{4}\right) \div \left(2 - \frac{1}{2}\right)$

Integers and fractions

Example 2.8 ▷ Work out each of the following.

a $\frac{3}{5} \times 15$ **b** $36 \times \frac{5}{8}$ **c** $\frac{3}{4}$ of 18

a This can be written as a multiplication of fractions. Any integer can be written as a fraction with a denominator of 1. You can then cancel.

$$\frac{3}{5} \times 15 = \frac{3}{\cancel{5}_{1}} \times \frac{\cancel{15}^{3}}{1} = 3 \times 3 = 9$$

b Following part **a**, you have:

$$36 \times \frac{5}{8} = \frac{\cancel{36}^{9}}{1} \times \frac{5}{\cancel{8}_{2}} = \frac{9}{1} \times \frac{5}{2} = \frac{45}{2} = 22\frac{1}{2}$$

c This can be done either as $\frac{3}{4} \times 18$ or as $\frac{1}{4}$ of $18 = 4\frac{1}{2}$, and the answer $\left(4\frac{1}{2}\right)$ multiplied by 3.

So, you have $\frac{3}{4}$ of $18 = 3 \times 4\frac{1}{2} = 13\frac{1}{2}$.

Example 2.9 ▷ Work out each of the following.

a How many thirds are there in two? **b** $4 \div \frac{1}{5}$.

a There are three thirds in one. So, there are $2 \times 3 = 6$ thirds in two.

b This can be done either as 'How many fifths in four?' or as a fraction division.

$$4 \div \frac{1}{5} = \frac{4}{1} \div \frac{1}{5} = \frac{4}{1} \times \frac{5}{1} = \frac{20}{1} = 20$$

Exercise 2D

1 In the following 12 cards are three sets of equivalent cards. Match them up.

| $\frac{2}{3}$ of 12 | $\frac{3}{8}$ of 16 | 12 | $16 \times \frac{3}{8}$ | 6 | 8 |

| $16 \times \frac{3}{4}$ | $\frac{3}{4}$ of 16 | $12 \times \frac{2}{3}$ | $\frac{3}{8} \times 16$ | $\frac{3}{4} \times 16$ | $\frac{2}{3} \times 12$ |

2 If $\frac{3}{4} \times 20 = 15$, which of these are true and which are false?

a $\frac{3}{4} \times 40 = 7.5$ **b** $\frac{3}{8} \times 20 = 30$ **c** $\frac{1}{4} \times 20 = 5$

d $\frac{1}{4} \times 20 = 45$ **e** $\frac{3}{4} \times 40 = 30$ **f** $\frac{3}{8} \times 20 = 7.5$

3 If $\frac{2}{3} \times x = 10$, copy and fill in each of the missing numbers.

    a $\frac{2}{3} \times 2x = \dots$ **b** $\frac{1}{3} \times x = \dots$ **c** $x = \dots$

4 Copy and fill in each of the missing numbers.

$\frac{1}{5} \times 2 = \frac{2}{5}$	$\frac{4}{5} \times 2 = \frac{8}{5}$	$\frac{2}{7} \times 2 = \frac{4}{7}$
$\frac{1}{5} \times 3 = \frac{3}{5}$	$\frac{4}{5} \times 3 = \dots$	$\frac{3}{7} \times 2 = \dots$
$\frac{1}{5} \times 4 = \dots$	$\frac{4}{5} \times 4 = \dots$	$\frac{4}{7} \times 5 = \dots$
$\frac{1}{5} \times 8 = \dots$	$\frac{4}{5} \times 8 = \dots$	$\frac{5}{7} \times 3 = \dots$
$\dots \times 10 = 2$	$\dots \times 20 = 8$	$\dots \times 4 = \frac{24}{7}$

5 Work out each of the following. Write each integer as a fraction with a denominator of 1 and cancel to simplify the calculation.

    a $\frac{4}{9} \times 12$ **b** $\frac{3}{5} \times 20$ **c** $\frac{5}{12} \times 24$ **d** $\frac{5}{8} \times 28$

    e $15 \times \frac{7}{12}$ **f** $\frac{8}{9} \times 15$ **g** $24 \times \frac{7}{15}$ **h** $\frac{5}{18} \times 24$

6  $4 \div \frac{1}{4} = 16$  $4 \div \frac{1}{4} = 1$

Who is correct? Explain why.

7 Write down the answer to each of the following.

    a $5 \div \frac{1}{3}$ **b** $4 \div \frac{1}{2}$ **c** $6 \div \frac{1}{4}$ **d** $2 \div \frac{1}{8}$

    e $6 \div \frac{1}{4}$ **f** $8 \div \frac{1}{9}$ **g** $5 \div \frac{1}{9}$ **h** $3 \div \frac{1}{5}$

8   **a**   How many thirds are there in 20?   **b**   How many halves are there in six?

        c   How many quarters are there in 15?   **d**   How many fifths are there in ten?

Extension Work

The factors of 120 are {1, 2, 3, 4, 5, 6, 8, 10, 12, 15, 20, 24, 30, 40, 60, 120}.

Look at the following calculations.

     $120 \times \frac{1}{8} = 15$ $60 \times \frac{2}{8} = 15$ $40 \times \frac{3}{8} = 15$ $30 \times \frac{4}{8} = 15$

Copy and complete these statements.

a   The answer is always ……

b   The denominator of the fraction is always ……

c   The starting integer and the numerator have a product of ……

Copy and complete each of these calculations.

d   **i**   …… $\times \frac{5}{8} = 15$ **ii** $20 \times \frac{\dots}{8} = 15$ **iii**   …… $\times \frac{1}{8} = 15$

e   The factors of 24 are {1, 2, 3, 4, 6, 8, 12, 24}.

Copy the calculation below four times and fill it with four different pairs of numbers from the list of factors to make it true.

     …… $\times \frac{\dots}{6} = 4$

Ratio

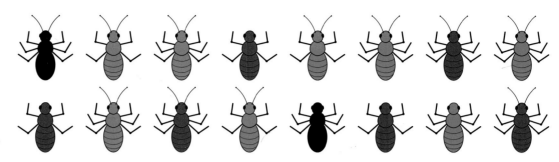

What is the ratio of blue bugs to red bugs to black bugs? What is the ratio of four-legged to six-legged bugs? What is the ratio of bugs with antennae to bugs without antennae?

You last had to deal with ratios of numbers in Year 7. This section will give you the chance to revise ratios and to take the ideas which you met then a step further.

Example 2.10 Simplify each of the following ratios.

    a $14 : 16$ **b** $0.2 : 3$ **c** $1.5 : 0.5$

    a Divide each number by the HCF (in this case 2). This gives $14 : 16 = 7 : 8$.

    b Ratios should not contain decimals unless they are in the form shown in Example 2.11. So, multiply by 5 to get rid of the decimal. This gives $0.2 : 3 = 1 : 15$.

    c In this case, multiply by 2 to get rid of the decimal. The resulting ratio can be cancelled if necessary. This gives $1.5 : 0.5 = 3 : 1$.

Example 2.11 Write each of the following in the form **i** $1 : m$ and **ii** $n : 1$.

    a $5 : 8$ **b** $7 : 10$ **c** $2 : 25$

    a **i** To get in the form $1 : m$, divide $5 : 8$ by the first number, in this case 5. This gives $1 : 1.6$.

        ii To get in the form $n : 1$, divide $5 : 8$ by the second number, in this case 8. This gives $0.625 : 1$.

    b **i** Divide $7 : 10$ by 7, which gives $1 : 1.43$ (rounded to two dp).

        ii Divide $7 : 10$ by 10, which gives $0.7 : 1$.

    c **i** Divide $2 : 25$ by 2, which gives $1 : 12.5$.

        ii Divide $2 : 25$ by 25, which gives $0.08 : 1$.

Example 2.12 Divide £150 in the ratio $2 : 3$.

The ratio $2 : 3$ means that £150 is first divided into $2 + 3$ equal parts. That is, 5 parts = £150, which gives 1 part = £150 ÷ 5 = £30.

Hence, you have:

    2 parts = £60
    3 parts = £90

which give the ratio £60 : £90.

1 Cancel each of the following ratios to its simplest form.

    a   4 : 12   **b**   10 : 15   **c**   8 : 16   **d**   5 : 15   **e**   25 : 40

    f   4 : 16   **g**   15 : 50   **h**   9 : 27   **i**   4 : 16 : 20   **j**   10 : 15 : 25

2 Write each of the following ratios in the form $1 : n$.

    a   4 : 16   **b**   5 : 16   **c**   8 : 20   **d**   6 : 15   **e**   5 : 40

    f   2 : 3   **g**   4 : 10   **h**   9 : 27   **i**   24 : 72   **j**   30 : 45

3 Write each of the following ratios in the form $n : 1$.

    a   16 : 2   **b**   10 : 2   **c**   8 : 10   **d**   9 : 5   **e**   25 : 10

    f   4 : 16   **g**   5 : 10   **h**   9 : 12   **i**   6 : 12   **j**   15 : 25

4 The proportion of gold to base metals in two alloys used to make jewellery are 6 : 5 and 11 : 10. By writing the two ratios in the form $1 : n$, state which has the greater proportion of gold.

5 In two sixth form maths classes, the ratios of the total number of students in each class to those with grade A at AS level are respectively 15 : 8 and 8 : 5. By writing the ratios in the form $n : 1$, state which class has the greater proportion of grade As.

6 **a**   Divide £300 in the ratio 3 : 2.   **b**   Divide £200 in the ratio 3 : 7.

   c   Divide £800 in the ratio 1 : 7.   **d**   Divide £450 in the ratio 4 : 1.

7 A recipe for pastry uses two cups of flour to half a cup of margarine. How much flour will be needed to make 500 grams of pastry?

8 A concrete mix is made from cement, gravel, sharp sand and builder's sand in the ratio 2 : 4 : 3 : 5.

How much cement will be needed to mix with 35 kg of builder's sand?

9 To make dark green paint 2 parts of yellow paint are mixed with 5 parts of blue. I have 250 ml of yellow and 1 litre of blue. What is the maximum amount of dark green paint I can make?

Extension Work

These three blocks are **similar**. That means that their shapes are the same but of different sizes.

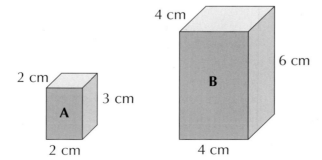
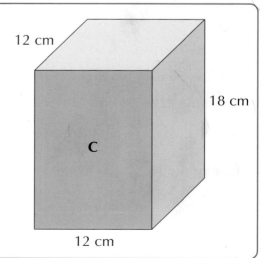

a The area of the front face of block A is 6 cm². Work out the area of the front face of the other two blocks.

b The volume of block A is 12 cm³. Work out the volume of the other two blocks.

Next, work out each of the following ratios and write each ratio in the form 1 : n.

c **i** Length of block A to length of block B.
   ii Area of the front face of block A to area of front face of block B.
  iii Volume of block A to volume of block B.

d **i** Length of block A to length of block C.
   ii Area of the front face of block A to area of front face of block C.
  iii Volume of block A to volume of block C.

e **i** Length of block B to length of block C.
   ii Area of front face of block B to area of front face of block C.
  iii Volume of block B to volume of block C.

Look at the answers to parts **c**, **d** and **e**. What do you notice?

Direct proportion

Example 2.13

Six tubes of toothpaste have a total mass of 900 grams. What is the mass of five tubes?

If six tubes have a mass of 900 grams, one tube has a mass of 900 ÷ 6 = 150 grams.

Hence, five tubes have a mass of 5 × 150 = 750 grams.

Example 2.14

A boy saves the same amount of money each week. In eight weeks he saves £20.

a How long will it take him to save £35?

b How much will he save in 10 weeks?

a If the boy saves £20 in 8 weeks, he saves £20 ÷ 8 = £2.50 in one week.

Hence, to save £35, he takes £35 ÷ £2.50 = 14 weeks.

b In 10 weeks he saves 10 × £2.50 = £25.

Example 2.15

A guitarist plays for 40 minutes with 400 people in the audience. How long would it take him to play the same set if there were only 300 people in the audience?

It takes exactly the same time of 40 minutes! The number of people in the audience does not affect the length of the performance.

Be careful. Some of these questions may trip you up!

1 In 5 hours, a man earns £30. How much does he earn in 6 hours?

2 A man walks 3 miles in 1 hour. How long would it take him to walk 5 miles?

3 Seven chocolate bars cost £1.40. How much do 10 chocolate bars cost?

4 In two days my watch loses 4 minutes. How much does it lose in one week (seven days)?

5 It takes 6 minutes to hard-boil three eggs in a pan. How long would it take to hard-boil two eggs in the same pan?

6 3 kg of rice cost £1.80. How much would 4 kg of rice cost?

7 Four packets of Smartoes sweets cost 88p. How much would three packets of Smartoes cost?

8 In 20 minutes an aircraft travels 180 miles. How far would it travel in 25 minutes at the same speed?

9 The cost of hiring a car for 12 days is £180. How much would it cost to hire the car for 5 days?

10 Four buckets standing in a rain shower take 40 minutes to fill. How long would three buckets standing in the same rain shower take to fill?

11 A distance of 8 km is represented by a distance of 16 cm on a map.

   a How many centimetres would represent a distance of 14 km?

   b What distance is represented by 7 cm on the map?

12 My motorbike travels 120 miles on 10 litres of petrol.

   a How many miles will it travel on 12 litres?

   b How many litres will I need to travel 30 miles?

13 An electric lamp uses 4 units of electricity in 120 minutes. If 9 units of electricity have been used, how long has it been switched on?

14 Nine washing-up liquid containers hold 2700 cm³. How much do five of these containers hold?

15 It takes 12 seconds to dial the 12-digit number of a friend who lives 100 miles away.

   a   How long will it take to dial the 12-digit number of a friend who lives 50 miles away?

   b   How long will it take to dial the 6-digit number of a friend who lives 10 miles away?

16 My washing machine takes 1 hour to wash a load that weighs 6 kg. How long will it take to wash a load that weighs 5 kg?

17 It takes John a week to read a book of 350 pages. How long will it take him to read a book of 200 pages?

18 With 120 passengers on board, a train takes 16 minutes to travel between two stations. How long would it take with only 60 passengers on board?

19 Six peaches cost 84p. How much will nine peaches cost?

20 A carpet whose area is 15 m² costs £120. How much would a carpet cost whose area is 20 m²?

Extension Work

You are told that

$a \times b \times c = 100$

a   What would the answer be if *a* were doubled?

b   What would the answer be if *b* were trebled?

c   What would the answer be if *c* were halved?

d   What would the answer be if *a* were doubled, *b* were trebled and *c* were halved at the same time?

e   What would the answer be if *a* were doubled, *b* were doubled and *c* were doubled at the same time?

f   What would the answer be if *a* were halved, *b* were halved and *c* were halved at the same time?

Inverse proportion

Example 2.16 ▷ Six teenagers take four days to paint a fence. How long will it take eight teenagers?

Six teenagers paint the fence in four days, so one teenager would paint the fence in 6 × 4 = 24 days.

Hence, eight teenagers would paint the fence in 24 ÷ 8 = 3 days.

Example 2.17 ▷ At 40 mph, it takes a train 3 hours to cover a certain distance. How long would it take to cover the same distance at 60 mph?

The distance travelled is 40 × 3 = 120 miles.

Hence, at 60 mph the train would take 120 ÷ 60 = 2 hours.

Example 2.18 ▷ Six shirts hanging on a washing line take 2 hours to dry.

How long would it take three shirts to dry?

It would take the same time! The number of shirts on the line does not make any difference.

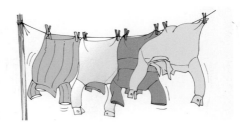

Exercise 2G

Be careful. Some of these questions may trip you up!

Use of a calculator is allowed for this exercise.

1 Four people lay a pipeline in 5 days. How long would ten people take?
2.5 days

2 Travelling at 8 miles per hour, a man takes 5 hours for a cycling trip. How long would he take at a speed of 10 miles per hour?
3

3 Two decorators can paint a room in 6 hours. How long would three decorators take?

4 A shelf is filled with 20 books, each 3 cm thick. If the books are replaced with 30 books of equal thickness, how thick would they have to be to fill the shelf?

5 From the top of a hill, two walkers can see 20 miles. How far would three walkers be able to see from the top of the same hill?

6 Some cans of beans are packed into seven boxes, each of which holds 12 cans. If I pack them into six boxes instead, how many cans will be in each box?

7 I have three cats who eat a large bag of cat food between them every four days. If I get another cat, how long will the bag of food last now?

8 Nine people build a wall in 20 days. How long will the job take 18 people?

9 Eggs laid by my chickens are packed into trays. With 24 eggs per tray, I need 10 trays. How many trays will I need when there are only 12 eggs per tray?

10 A secretary can type 15 pages, each of 60 lines, in one hour. If she had typed only 9 pages, how many lines would be on each page?

11 A lorry takes 8 hours to do a journey at a speed of 30 mph.

   a How long would the same journey take at 40 mph?

   b How fast would the lorry be travelling if the journey takes 10 hours?

12 Six horses eat 10 bags of hay every 2 days.

   a How many days would 10 bags of hay last four horses?

   b How many days would 20 bags of hay last 12 horses?

13 At £25 a week, it would take Dave 20 weeks to pay off his debts.

   a How long would it take him to pay off his debts at £50 a week?

   b How much would he have to pay weekly to pay off his debts over 40 weeks?

14 If I spend £15 a day, my money will last me 10 days. If I spend £12.50 a day, how long will my money last?

15 When I use 2 grams of toothpaste, I take 2 minutes to brush my teeth. How long will it take me to brush my teeth if I use 3 grams of toothpaste?

16 Four taps fill a bath in 30 minutes. How long would it take three taps to fill the same bath?

17 At peak times, a phone card gives 120 minutes of calls. At off-peak times, the cost is one-third of the cost at peak times. How many minutes of calls will the phone card give at off-peak times?

18 A box of emergency rations can feed 12 people for 6 days. How long would the box of rations last 8 people?

19 It takes someone 10 minutes to hang out a load of washing. How long would it take two people?

20 One man went to mow a meadow. It took him 15 minutes to walk there. If two men went to mow a meadow how long would it take them to walk there?

a Two fences posts are 10 metres apart.

If three posts are spaced equally between them, the gap between each post will be 2.5 metres.

    i How large will the gap be between each post if five posts are equally spaced between the two outer posts?

    ii How large will the gap be between each post if nine posts are equally spaced between the two outer posts?

b Two posts are 12 metres apart. How many posts would need to be placed between them so that they end up 2 metres apart?

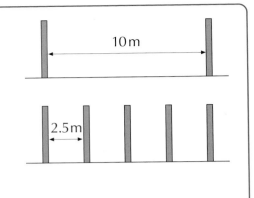

Rounding and calculator displays

Example 2.19 ▷ Round each of these numbers to   **i** one decimal place   **ii** two decimal places.

    a 7.822   **b** 8.565   **c** 9.018

    a **i**   7.8 to one decimal place   **ii**   7.82 to two decimal places

    b **i**   8.6 to one decimal place   **ii**   8.57 to two decimal places

    c **i**   9.0 to one decimal place   **ii**   9.02 to two decimal places

Example 2.20 ▷ Look at the two calculator displays. What numbers do they represent?

    a 4.6^{02} means $4.6 \times 100 = 460$

    b $8.6^{\,-03}$ means $8.6 \div 1000 = 0.0086$

Exercise 2H

1 Round these numbers to one decimal place.

    a 2.34   **b** 4.57   **c** 3.68   **d** 7.89   **e** 2.09

    f 3.12   **g** 4.58   **h** 3.24   **i** 4.71   **j** 4.55

2 Round these numbers to two decimal places.

    a 2.364   **b** 4.348   **c** 3.231   **d** 7.812

    e 2.092   **f** 3.222   **g** 8.436   **h** 5.678

3 a   Write out in full the number shown on this calculator display.

b   Write out in full the number shown on this calculator display.

4   Liam thought that when the number 1.24^{03} was written out in full, it would have three zeros in it. Gary said that it would have only one zero. Who, if anybody, is right? What is the number written out in full?

5   Which of these numbers is equal to a calculator display of 3.4^{03}?

    a   3.4000   **b**   3400   **c**   34 000   **d**   0.000 34

6   Which of these numbers is equal to a calculator display of 5.6^{-02}?

    a   0.5600   **b**   0.0056   **c**   0.056   **d**   0.56

7   Write down the value shown by each of these calculator displays.

    a 4.3^{02} **b** 5.8^{03} **c** 6.9^{02} **d** 2.5^{04}

8   Write down the value shown by each of these calculator displays.

    a 5.7^{-02} **b** 1.7^{-03} **c** 9.8^{-02} **d** 6.2^{-04}

9   Write each of these numbers as a calculator display.

    a   5400   **b**   2100   **c**   480   **d**   83 000

10   Write each of these numbers as a calculator display.

    a   0.072   **b**   0.0021   **c**   0.059   **d**   0.006 72

Extension Work

Find out which button on your calculator lets you key in displays like the ones you have looked at this lesson.

What is the biggest number that you can key in to the calculator?

What you need to know for level 4

- Be able to recognise simple fractions and their decimal and percentage equivalents
- How to add and subtract simple fractions and fractions with the same denominator
- Be able to order decimal numbers with up to two decimal places

What you need to know for level 5

- How to multiply and divide decimal numbers by 10, 100 and 1000
- How to reduce a fraction to its lowest term by cancelling common factors in its numerator and denominator
- How to solve problems which involve ratio and direct proportion

National Curriculum SATs questions

LEVEL 4

1 *1999 Paper 2*

Here are some number cards:

$$\boxed{1} \quad \boxed{7} \quad \boxed{3} \quad \boxed{5}$$

You can use each card once to make the number 1735, like this:

$$\boxed{1}\boxed{7}\boxed{3}\boxed{5}$$

Use the four number cards to make numbers that are as close as possible to the numbers written below.

Example:

8000 $\longrightarrow$ $\boxed{7}\boxed{5}\boxed{3}\boxed{1}$

You must not use the same card more than once in each answer.

4000 $\longrightarrow$ $\boxed{}\boxed{}\boxed{}\boxed{}$

1500 $\longrightarrow$ $\boxed{}\boxed{}\boxed{}\boxed{}$

1600 $\longrightarrow$ $\boxed{}\boxed{}\boxed{}\boxed{}$

2 *1998 Paper 1*

Here are the ingredients for 1 fruit cake.

One fruit cake	**Ten fruit cakes**
200 g self-raising flour	2000 g = 2 kg self-raising flour
100 g caster sugar	...... g = ... kg caster sugar
150 g margarine	...... g = ... kg margarine
125 g mixed fruit	...... g = ... kg mixed fruit
3 eggs	30 eggs

a Copy and complete the table to show how much of each ingredient you need to make ten fruit cakes. Give your answers in grams and in kilograms

b Six eggs cost 70p. How much will 30 eggs cost?

LEVEL 5

3 *1998 Paper 2*

You can make different colours of paint by mixing red, blue and yellow in different proportions.

For example, you can make green by mixing 1 part blue to 1 part yellow.

a To make purple, you mix 3 parts red to 7 parts blue. How much of each colour do you need to make 20 litres of purple paint? Give your answer in litres.

b To make orange, you mix 13 parts yellow to 7 parts red. How much of each colour do you need to make 10 litres of orange paint? Give your answer in litres.

4 *1999 Paper 2*

a Nigel pours one carton of apple juice and three cartons of orange juice into a big jug.

What is the ratio of apple juice to orange juice in Nigel's jug?

b Lesley pours one carton of apple juice and $1\frac{1}{2}$ cartons of orange juice into another big jug.

What is the ratio of apple juice to orange juice in Lesley's jug?

c Tandi pours one carton of apple juice and one carton of orange juice into another big jug.

She wants only half as much apple juice as orange juice in her jug. What should Tandi pour into her jug now?

This chapter is going to show you

- how to work out formulae
- how to find inverse functions
- how to solve linear equations including those with unknowns on both sides
- how to construct equations to help solve problems
- how graphs can be used to help solve problems

What you should already know

- How to draw a mapping diagram
- How to solve simple linear equations
- How to plot points and draw a straight-line graph

Formulae

A **formula** is a rule used to work out a value from one or more values (called **variables** or **inputs**). For example, $A = ab$ is a rule, or formula, used to calculate the area, A, of a rectangle from the lengths, a and b, of two adjacent sides.

'What is the difference between a function and a formula?'

'The way it's written down. They are the same thing really, except that a function usually has only one input whereas a formula often has more than one input.'

A formula also always has a **subject** (an output), which is usually written on the left-hand side of the equals sign. For example:

$$P = 2a + 2b$$

The output is P.   Inputs are a and b.

This is also called the subject of the formula.

When a is 3 cm and b is 5 cm, the formula becomes:

$P = 2 \times 3 + 2 \times 5$
  $= 16$ cm

Exercise 3A

1 The formula $C = 3D$ is used to calculate approximately the circumference, C, of a circle from its diameter, D. Use the formula to calculate the approximate circumference of each circle shown below.

a  4 cm

b 2 cm

c  13 cm

2 The formula $A = 180n - 360$ is used to calculate the sum of the angles inside a polygon with n sides. Use the formula to calculate the sum of the angles inside each polygon shown below.

    a   Pentagon, five sides   **b**   Hexagon, six sides

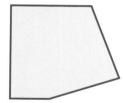 

3 The cost, C, of placing an advertisement in a local newspaper is given by:

$$C = £20 + £2N$$

where N is the number of words used in the advertisement.

What is the cost of placing each of the following advertisements?

    a   With 12 words.

    b   With 25 words.

4 Lennie, the driving instructor, used the following formula to charge learner drivers:

$$C = £4 + £13H$$

where H is the number of hours in the driving lesson.

What is the cost of each of the following driving lessons?

    a   One lasting 2 hours.

    b   One lasting from 1 pm to 4 pm.

5 The amount of money, M, expected to be collected for a charity was approximated by the following formula:

$$M = £5000T + £20C$$

where T is the number of TV advertisements appearing the day before a charity event was held, and C is the number of collectors.

Approximately, how much is expected to be collected by each of the following charities?

    a   NCS had three TV advertisements and 100 collectors.

    b   TTU had two TV advertisements and 300 collectors.

    c   BCB had no TV advertisements and 500 collectors.

6 The speed, S m/s, of a rocket can be found from the formula $S = AT$, where the rocket has acceleration, A m/s^2, for a number of seconds, T.

Find the speed of a rocket in each of the following cases.

    a   The rocket has an acceleration of 25 m/s^2 for 8 seconds.

    b   The rocket has an acceleration of 55 m/s^2 for 6 seconds.

7 The formula $a = \frac{1}{2}bh$ is used to calculate the area, a, of a triangle from its base length, b, and its height, h. Use the formula to calculate the area of each triangle shown below.

a
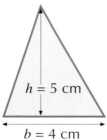
$h = 5$ cm
$b = 4$ cm

b
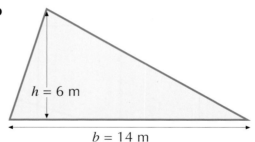
$h = 6$ m
$b = 14$ m

8 MC Dave used the following formula to calculate the cost, C, of his gigs:

$$C = £55 + £3N + £5T + £10E$$

where:

    N is the number of people attending the gig.

    T is the number of hours worked before midnight.

    E is the number of hours worked after midnight.

Calculate the cost of each of the following gigs.

a With 60 people attending from 9 pm to 2 am.

b With 40 people from 7 pm to 1 am.

Extension Work

The function $x \rightarrow \dfrac{3x + 5}{4}$ can be worked through with the following flow chart.

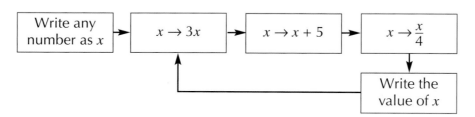

a Show that starting with $x = 9$, the flow chart gives the following result.

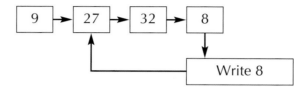

b Continue to work through the flow chart at least ten times.

c What do you notice?

d Does the value of the starting number make any difference?

Inverse functions

Every linear function has an **inverse function** which reverses the direction of the operation. In other words, the output is brought back to the input.

Example 3.1

The inverse function of $x \to 3x$ can be shown to be $x \to \frac{x}{3}$

$$x \to 3x$$
$$0 \to 0 \to 0$$
$$1 \to 3 \to 1$$
$$2 \to 6 \to 2$$
$$3 \to 9 \to 3$$
$$x \to \frac{x}{3}$$

Hence, the inverse function is:

$$x \to \frac{x}{3}$$

Example 3.2

The inverse function of $x \to x + 4$ can be shown to be $x \to x - 4$

$$x \to x + 4$$
$$0 \to \quad 4 \to 0$$
$$1 \to \quad 5 \to 1$$
$$2 \to \quad 6 \to 2$$
$$3 \to \quad 7 \to 3$$
$$x \to x - 4$$

Hence, the inverse function is:

$$x \to x - 4$$

When a function is built up from two or more operations, you have to use the inverse function of each operation and work back through them to find the overall inverse function.

Example 3.3

Find the inverse function of $x \to 4x + 3$.

The sequence of operations for this function is:

Input $\longrightarrow$ $\boxed{\times 4}$ $\longrightarrow$ $\boxed{+ 3}$ $\longrightarrow$ Output

Reversing this sequence gives:

Output $\longleftarrow$ $\boxed{\div 4}$ $\longleftarrow$ $\boxed{- 3}$ $\longleftarrow$ Input

Next, give the input the value x:

$$\frac{x - 3}{4} \leftarrow x - 3 \leftarrow x$$

So, the inverse function is:

$$x \to \frac{x - 3}{4}$$

The inverse function of some functions are the functions themselves, as Example 3.4 shows.

Example 3.4 ▷ The inverse function of $x \to 9 - x$ can be shown to be the function itself. That is, $x \to 9 - x$. That is,

$$x \to 9 - x$$
$$0 \to \quad 9 \to 0$$
$$1 \to \quad 8 \to 1$$
$$2 \to \quad 7 \to 2$$
$$3 \to \quad 6 \to 3$$
$$x \to 9 - x$$

Hence, the inverse function is the function itself.

Exercise 3B

1 Write down the inverse function of each of the following functions.

   a $x \to 5x$ **b** $x \to 4x$ **c** $x \to x + 1$

   d $x \to x + 7$ **e** $x \to x - 2$ **f** $x \to \frac{x}{2}$

2 Write down the inverse function of each of the following functions.

   a $x \to 2x + 5$ **b** $x \to 3x + 2$ **c** $x \to 4x - 1$

   d $x \to 5x - 3$ **e** $x \to 4x + 6$ **f** $x \to 6x - 2$

3

'I have a rule for any number they give me. It's multiply by 5 and add on 3.'

   a   Write down Joy's rule as a function.

   b   Write down the inverse function of Joy's function.

   c   Use the inverse function to find what number was given to Joy when she gave the reply '43'.

'I have a rule for any number they give me. It's add on 4 then multiply by 3.'

   d   Write down Dave's rule as a function.

   e   Write down the inverse function of Dave's function.

   f   Use the inverse function to find what number was given to Dave when he gave the reply '36'.

4 Write down the inverse function of each of the following functions.

   a $x \to 10 - 2x$ **b** $x \to 15 - 3x$ **c** $x \to 100 - 5x$

Find the inverse function of each of the following functions.

a $\quad x \to \dfrac{2x + 3}{4}$ b $\quad x \to \dfrac{3x - 4}{5}$ c $\quad x \to \dfrac{5x + 3}{2}$

d $\quad x \to \dfrac{4x - 2}{3}$ e $\quad x \to \dfrac{2x + 3}{7}$ f $\quad x \to \dfrac{7x + 2}{5}$

g $\quad x \to \dfrac{20 - 4x}{5}$ h $\quad x \to \dfrac{120 - 10x}{4}$ i $\quad x \to \dfrac{200 - 9x}{10}$

Solving equations

You have already met a few different types of equation, which were solved by using a flow diagram. Here, you are going to be shown how to solve them by adding, subtracting, multiplying or dividing both sides of an equation by the same number. The aim is to get the variable (usually x) on its own.

Example 3.5

Solve the equation $2x = 16$.

Divide both sides by 2, to give: $\dfrac{2x}{2} = \dfrac{16}{2}$

which gives: $x = 8$

So, the solution is $x = 8$.

Example 3.6

Solve the equation $4t + 3 = 23$.

Subtract 3 from both sides, to give: $4t + 3 - 3 = 23 - 3$

which gives: $4t = 20$

Divide both sides by 4, to give: $t = 5$

So, the solution is $t = 5$.

Example 3.7

Solve the equation $3x - 4 = 14$.

Add 4 to both sides, to give: $3x - 4 + 4 = 14 + 4$

which gives: $3x = 18$

Divide both sides by 3, to give: $x = 6$

So, the solution is $x = 6$.

Exercise 3C

In each of the following questions, show your working. Write each step on a new line.

1 Solve each of the following equations.

a $\quad 2x = 10$ b $\quad 3x = 12$ c $\quad 5x = 30$ d $\quad 4x = 28$

e $\quad 5t = 60$ f $\quad 7m = 21$ g $\quad 3k = 18$ h $\quad 2p = 36$

2 Solve each of the following equations.

a $3x + 5 = 11$	**b** $2x + 3 = 11$	**c** $4x + 7 = 15$
d $5x + 3 = 18$	**e** $3x + 4 = 19$	**f** $6x + 1 = 25$
g $2x + 7 = 15$	**h** $4x + 3 = 27$	**i** $3x + 6 = 27$
j $7p + 3 = 31$	**k** $2q + 1 = 19$	**l** $4b + 5 = 17$

3 Solve each of the following equations.

a $5x - 2 = 13$	**b** $3x - 4 = 11$	**c** $6x - 1 = 23$
d $2x - 3 = 11$	**e** $4x - 3 = 25$	**f** $3x - 2 = 22$
g $4x - 5 = 3$	**h** $6x - 1 = 17$	**i** $5x - 3 = 17$
j $2n - 5 = 9$	**k** $3w - 7 = 8$	**l** $7y - 2 = 19$

4 Solve each of the following equations.

a $3x = 18$	**b** $4x = 20$	**c** $6x = 24$
d $4x + 3 = 23$	**e** $3x + 2 = 14$	**f** $5x + 4 = 19$
g $4x - 1 = 19$	**h** $2x - 3 = 17$	**i** $5x - 4 = 21$
j $3m - 5 = 7$	**k** $4b + 5 = 17$	**l** $6q + 1 = 31$

5 Nazia has made a mistake somewhere in her working for each of the equations shown below. Can you spot the line on which the error occurs and work out the correct solution?

a
$$3x + 8 = 23$$
$$3x + 8 - 8 = 23 - 8$$
$$3x = 18$$
$$\frac{3x}{3} = \frac{18}{3}$$
$$x = 6 \quad ✗$$

b
$$5x - 3 = 22$$
$$3 - 5x - 3 = 22 + 3$$
$$-5x = 25$$
$$\frac{-5x}{-5} = \frac{25}{-5}$$
$$x = -5 \quad ✗$$

c
$$9 - 5x = 24$$
$$9 + 5x - 9 = 24 - 9$$
$$5x = 15$$
$$\frac{5x}{5} = \frac{15}{5}$$
$$x = 3 \quad ✗$$

d
$$2x - 5 = 17$$
$$2x - 5 + 5 = 17 + 5$$
$$2x = 12$$
$$\frac{2x}{2} = \frac{12}{2}$$
$$x = 6 \quad ✗$$

Extension Work

1 Solve each of the following equations. (All the answers are negative numbers.)

a $2x + 10 = 4$	**b** $3x + 9 = 3$	**c** $4x + 15 = 7$
d $3x + 11 = 2$	**e** $5x + 21 = 6$	**f** $2x + 17 = 5$

2 Solve each of the following equations. (All the answers are decimal numbers.)

a $4x + 3 = 13$	**b** $5x + 2 = 8$	**c** $2x + 1 = 8$
d $5x - 4 = 8$	**e** $2x - 5 = 12$	**f** $4x - 3 = 11$

Constructing equations to solve problems

The first step to solve a problem using algebra is to write down an equation. This is called constructing an equation. To do this, you must choose a letter to stand for the simplest variable (unknown) in the problem. This might be x or the first letter of a suitable word. For example, n is often used to stand for the number.

Example 3.8 ▶

My son is 25 years younger than I am. Our ages add up to 81. How old are we?

Construct the equation using x as my son's age. (Since this is the lower age.)

So, my age is $x + 25$.

The total of our ages is 81, which gives:

$$x + x + 25 = 81$$

This simplifies to:

$$2x + 25 = 81$$

Subtract 25 from both sides, to give:

$$2x = 56$$
$$x = 28 \quad \text{(Divide through by 2.)}$$

So, my son's age is 28 years, and I am 25 years older, aged 53.

Exercise 3D

1 Tom has 10 more marbles than Jeff.
Together they have 56.

   a Write down an equation which this gives.

   b Solve the equation to find the number of marbles each boy has.

2 Sanjay has 35 more CDs than Surjit. Together they have 89 CDs.

   a Write down an equation which this gives.

   b Solve the equation to find the number of CDs they each have.

3 Gavin has 13 more DVDs than Michelle. Together they have 129 DVDs.

   a Write down an equation which this gives.

   b Solve the equation to find the number of DVDs they each have.

4 Joy thinks of a number rule.

   a When Paul gives Joy a number, she replies, '23'. Write down the equation this gives and solve it to find the number which Paul gave to Joy.

   b When Billie gives Joy a number, she replies, '38'. Write down the equation this gives and solve it to find the number which Billie gave to Joy.

'Multiply the number by 3 and add 5.'

5 Paula is three times as old as Angus. Their ages add up to 52.

    a Write down an equation which this gives.

    b Solve the equation to find both ages.

6 David scored twice as many goals in a season as Mark. Together, they scored 36 goals.

    a Write down an equation which this gives.

    b Solve the equation to find how many goals each player scored.

7 Alan spent four times as many minutes on his maths homework as he did on the rest of his homework. He spent two hours on his homework altogether.

    a Write down an equation which this gives.

    b Solve the equation to find out how much time Alan spent on his maths homework.

8 Farmer Giles keeps only sheep and cows on his farm. He has 55 more sheep than cows and has 207 animals altogether.

    a Write down an equation which this gives.

    b Solve the equation to find the number of sheep and the number of cows on Farmer Giles' farm.

9 In a school of 845 students, there are 29 more girls than boys.

    a Write down an equation which this gives.

    b Solve the equation to find the number girls and the number of boys in the school.

10 On an aircraft carrying 528 passengers, there were 410 more adults than children.

    a Write down an equation which this gives.

    b Solve the equation to find the number of children on this aircraft.

Extension Work

1 Two consecutive numbers add up to 77. What are the two numbers?

2 Two consecutive numbers add up to 135. What is the product of the two numbers?

3 What is the product of three consecutive numbers which add up to 402?

Equations with unknown quantities on both sides

When x is on both sides of the equals sign, your first step is to get rid of x from one side. You do this by adding or subtracting terms.

Example 3.9 ▷

Solve the equation $4x = 12 + x$.

Subtract x from both sides, to give:

$$4x - x = 12 + x - x$$

which simplifies to:

$$3x = 12$$
$$\frac{3x}{3} = \frac{12}{3} \quad \text{(Divide through by 3.)}$$
$$x = 4$$

So, the solution is $x = 4$.

Example 3.10 ▷

Solve the equation $6x + 5 = 2x + 33$.

Subtract $2x$ from both sides, to give:

$$6x + 5 - 2x = 2x + 33 - 2x$$

which simplifies to:

$$4x + 5 = 33$$

Now subtract 5 from both sides, to obtain:

$$4x = 28$$
$$\frac{4x}{4} = \frac{28}{4} \quad \text{(Divide through by 4.)}$$
$$x = 7$$

So, the solution is $x = 7$.

Example 3.11 ▷

Solve the equation $4x + 3 = 13 - x$.

Add x to both both sides, to give:

$$4x + 3 + x = 13 - x + x$$

which simplifies to:

$$5x + 3 = 13$$

Subtract 3 from both sides, to obtain:

$$5x = 10$$
$$\frac{5x}{5} = \frac{10}{5} \quad \text{(Divide through by 5.)}$$
$$x = 2$$

So, the solution is $x = 2$.

1 Solve each of the following equations.

a	$3x = 8 + x$	**b**	$4x = 15 + x$	**c**	$5x = 20 + x$	**d**	$6x = 25 + x$
e	$4x = 20 + 2x$	**f**	$6x = 12 + 2x$	**g**	$5x = 21 + 2x$	**h**	$6x = 32 + 2x$
i	$8x = 12 + 4x$	**j**	$5x = 16 + 3x$	**k**	$4x = 10 + 2x$	**l**	$8x = 30 + 5x$

2 Solve each of the following equations.

a	$4x + 3 = x + 15$	**b**	$3x + 4 = x + 20$	**c**	$5x + 3 = x + 19$
d	$5x - 2 = 2x + 10$	**e**	$6x - 3 = 2x + 9$	**f**	$5x - 6 = 3x + 14$
g	$7x - 19 = 2x - 4$	**h**	$6x - 10 = 3x - 1$	**i**	$7x + 2 = 4x + 8$

3 Solve each of the following equations.

a	$5x + 2 = 10 + x$	**b**	$7x + 5 = 17 + x$	**c**	$4x + 1 = 10 + x$
d	$7x - 3 = 12 + 2x$	**e**	$6x - 2 = 18 + 2x$	**f**	$5x - 5 = 7 + 2x$
g	$7 + 4x = 13 + 2x$	**h**	$7 + 4x = 11 + 2x$	**i**	$8 + 5x = 14 + 3x$

4 Solve each of the following equations.

a	$2x + 3 = 15 - x$	**b**	$3x + 5 = 25 - x$	**c**	$5x - 4 = 10 - 2x$
d	$5x - 10 = 6 - 3x$	**e**	$7x + 3 = 21 - 2x$	**f**	$9x - 10 = 23 - 2x$
g	$5x + 7 = 37 - x$	**h**	$7 + 4x = 49 - 2x$	**i**	$7x - 6 = 34 - 3x$

Extension Work

1 Solve each of the following equations. (All the answers are negative numbers.)

a	$3x + 8 = 4 + x$	**b**	$5x + 19 = 3 + x$	**c**	$6x + 11 = 1 + x$
d	$5x + 11 = 2 + 2x$	**e**	$6x + 21 = 5 - 2x$	**f**	$3x + 17 = 2 - 2x$

2 Solve each of the following equations. (All the answers are decimal numbers.)

a	$5x + 3 = 9 + x$	**b**	$4x + 2 = 7 + 2x$	**c**	$7x + 1 = 8 + 2x$
d	$3x - 4 = 7 - 2x$	**e**	$x - 5 = 14 - 3x$	**f**	$4x - 7 = 12 - 6x$

Problems involving straight-line graphs

When a car is being filled with petrol, both the amount and the cost of the petrol are displayed on the pump. One litre of petrol costs 80p. So, 2 litres cost 160p (£1.60) and 5 litres cost 400p (£4).

The table below shows the costs of different quantities of petrol as displayed on the pump.

Amount of petrol (litres)	5	10	15	20	25	30
Cost (£)	4.00	8.00	12.00	16.00	20.00	24.00

The information can be graphed, as shown on the right. Notice that for every 5 litres across the graph, the graph rises by £4. This is the reason why the graph is a straight line.

This idea can be used to solve a number of different types of problem.

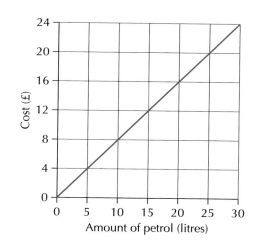

Example 3.12

Mr Evans wanted to convert all students' scores in a French test to percentages. He used the facts given on the right to help him to draw a conversion graph.

French score	0	60
Percentage	0	100

He used the above two points to draw a straight-line graph, as shown on the right.

Stephanie scored 30. Mr Evans used the graph to convert this score to 50%. Joe scored 38. Again using the graph, Mr Evans converted this to 63%.

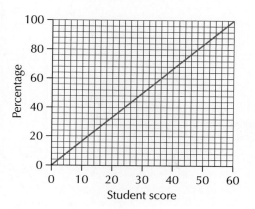

Exercise 3F

1 Jenny sold apples on a market stall. She was told just the following two prices.

Number of apples	0	12
Cost	£0	£1.50

a Plot the two points on a graph and join them with a straight line. Use the horizontal axis for the number of apples, going up to 20, and the vertical axis for the cost of apples, going up to £3.

b Use the graph to find the cost of each of the following.

   i 4 apples   ii 10 apples   iii 20 apples

c Use the graph to find how many apples you could buy for:

   i 75p   ii £1.75   iii £2.75

2 At a Joe King concert, fans can get posters of Joe from one of the stalls. Benny sells the posters and knows these facts about the costs:

Number of posters	0	20
Cost	£0	£17

a Plot the two points on a graph and join them with a straight line. Use the horizontal axis for the number of posters, and the vertical axis for the cost of posters, going up to £17.

b Use the graph to find the cost of each of the following.

    i 6 posters   **ii** 12 posters   **iii** 16 posters

c Use the graph to find how many posters you could buy for:

    i £6.80   **ii** £11.90   **iii** £15.30

3 Tom put a weight on the end of a spring to see how much it was stretched. After this, he knew these facts:

Weight (g)	0	900
Stretch (cm)	0	18

a Plot the two points on a graph and join them with a straight line. Use the horizontal axis for the weights added, going up to 1000 g, and the vertical axis for the stretch of the spring, going up to 20 cm.

b Use the graph to find the stretch of each of the following.

    i 200 grams   **ii** 300 grams   **iii** 1 kilogram

c Use the graph to find the weight needed to stretch the spring:

    i 2 cm   **ii** 5 cm   **iii** 14 cm

4 At a garden party, Kim looked after the hoopla stall. She knew two costs of the hooplas.

Number of hooplas	0	10
Cost	£0	£2.20

a Plot the two points on a graph and join them with a straight line. Use the horizontal axis for the numbers of hooplas, going up to 12, and the vertical axis for the cost of hooplas, going up to £3.

b Use the graph to find the cost of each of the following.

    i 3 hooplas   **ii** 8 hooplas   **iii** 12 hooplas

c Use the graph to find how many hooplas you get for:

    i 88p   **ii** £1.10   **iii** £2.42

5 Sue went to France for her holiday and knew the following facts about her British money and Euros.

British £	£0	£100
Euros €	€0	€160

a Plot the two points on a graph and join them with a straight line. Use the horizontal axis for British pounds, going up to £150, and the vertical axis for Euros, going up to €250.

b Use the graph to find the value in Euros of each of the following:

    i £20   **ii** £70   **iii** £130

c Use the graph to find the value in British £ for each of the following.

    i €40   **ii** €80   **iii** €232

Try to solve this problem by drawing a graph.

Two women are walking on the same long, straight road towards each other. One sets off at 9.00 am at a speed of 4 km/h. The other also sets off at 9.00 am, 15 km away, at a speed of 5 km/h.

a   At what time do the women meet?

b   How far will the first woman have walked when they meet?

What you need to know for level 4

- How to solve a simple equation
- Be able to plot a few points and draw a graph

What you need to know for level 5

- How to solve an equation with unknowns on both sides
- How to use a simple equation to solve a problem
- How to solve problems using graphs

National Curriculum SATs questions

LEVEL 4

1   *2002 Paper 1*

a   I can think of three different rules to change 6 to 18.

$$6 \rightarrow 18$$

Copy and complete these sentences to show what these rules could be.

First rule: add ......

Second rule: multiply by ......

Third rule: multiply by 2 then ......

b   Now I think of a new rule.

The new rule changes 10 to 5 and it changes 8 to 4.

$$10 \rightarrow 5$$ $$8 \rightarrow 4$$

Write what the new rule could be.

2 *1999 Paper 2*

The table shows the cost for an adult for one week in a holiday camp. It is for holidays between June and September in 1999.

Holidays starting between	Cost
June 5 – July 2	£85
July 3 – July 16	£105
July 17 – September 3	£130
September 4 – September 10	£90
September 11 – September 24	£75

a All the holidays start on a Saturday. The graph shows the cost of the holidays starting on each Saturday. Complete the graph for the last four weeks.

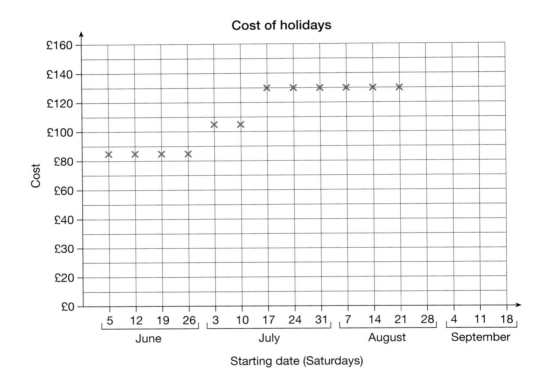

b What is the cost for an adult for one week in the holiday camp, beginning on August 14?

c The holidays cost more at some times than at others. Give a reason which could explain this difference.

d The cost in June for an adult for one week in the holiday camp is £85. The cost for a child is 25% less.

What is the cost in June for a child for one week in the holiday camp? Show your working.

What is the total cost for an adult and a child for one week in the holiday camp in June?

Child:
25% off
adult cost

3 *2002 Paper 1*

Look at this table:

Copy the table below and write in words the meaning of each equation. The first one is done for you.

	Age in years
Ann	a
Ben	b
Cindy	c

$b = 30$	Ben is 30 years old
$a + b = 69$	
$b = 2c$	
$\dfrac{a + b + c}{3} = 28$	

4 *2002 Paper 2*

A teacher has a large pile of cards.

An expression for the total number of cards is $6n + 8$.

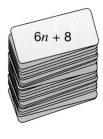

a The teacher puts the cards in two piles.

The number of cards in the first pile is $2n + 3$.

First pile   Second pile

Write an expression to show the number of cards in the second pile.

b The teacher puts all the cards together.

Then he uses them to make two equal piles.

Write an expression to show the number of cards in one of the piles.

c The teacher puts all the cards together again, then he uses them to make two piles.

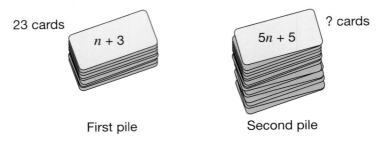

23 cards

$n + 3$

? cards

$5n + 5$

First pile   Second pile

There are 23 cards in the first pile.

How many cards are in the second pile? Show your working.

CHAPTER 4

Shape, Space and Measures 1

This chapter is going to show you

- how to identify alternate and corresponding angles
- how to calculate angles in triangles and quadrilaterals
- how to calculate the interior angles of polygons
- how regular polygons tessellate
- how to construct perpendicular bisectors and angle bisectors
- names of the different parts of a circle

What you should already know

- How to identify parallel and perpendicular lines
- How to measure and draw angles
- Interior angles of a triangle add up to 180°
- Names of polygons
- Be able to draw a circle given its radius

Alternate and corresponding angles

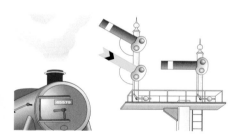

The diagram shows two parallel lines with another straight line cutting across them.

The line that cuts across a pair of parallel lines is called a **transversal**.

Notice that the transversal forms eight angles.

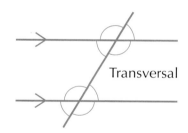

Alternate angles

Trace angle x on the diagram. Rotate your tracing paper through 180° and place angle x over angle y. What do you notice?

You should find that the two angles are the same size.

The two angles x and y are called **alternate angles**. (This is because they are on alternate sides of the transversal.) They are sometimes called Z-angles.

This shows that alternate angles are equal.

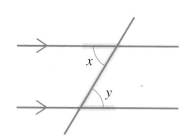

Example 4.1

Find the size of angle a on the diagram.

Alternate angles are equal, so $a = 120°$.

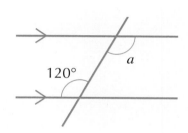

Trace angle x on the diagram. Slide your tracing paper along the transversal and place angle x over angle y. What do you notice?

You should find that the two angles are the same size.

The two angles, x and y, are called **corresponding angles**. (This is because the position of one angle corresponds to the position of the other.) They are sometimes called F-angles.

This shows that corresponding angles are equal.

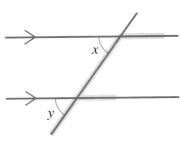

Example 4.2 ▷ Find the size of angle b and angle c on the diagram.

Corresponding angles are equal, so $b = 125°$.

Angles on a straight line add up to $180°$. Therefore, c is $180° - b$, which gives:

$$c = 180° - 125° = 55°$$

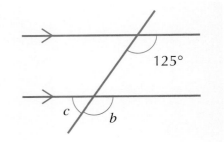

Exercise 4A

1 Work out the size of the lettered angle in each of these diagrams. State whether they are alternate angles or corresponding angles.

a
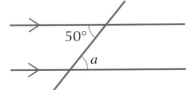

b
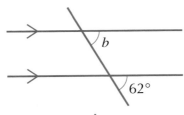

c
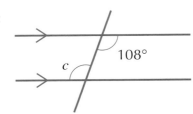

d
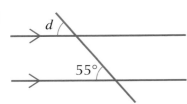

e
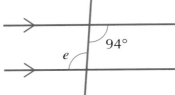

f
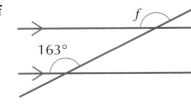

2 Work out the size of the lettered angles in each of these diagrams. Give an explanation of how you found each angle.

a
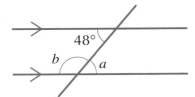

b
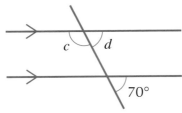

c
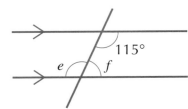

d
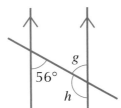

e
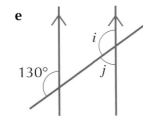

3 Alternate angles are sometimes called Z-angles. Draw suitable diagrams to explain why.

4 Corresponding angles are sometimes called F-angles. Draw suitable diagrams to explain why.

Work out the size of the lettered angles in each of these diagrams.

1

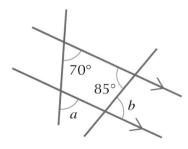

2

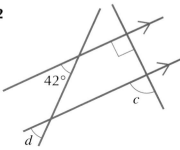

3

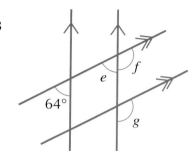

4

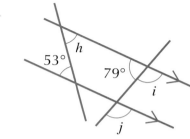

Angles of a triangle

You already know that the sum of the interior angles of a triangle is 180°. In the diagram:

$a + b + c = 180°$

Example 4.3 shows you how to find an **exterior angle** of a triangle.

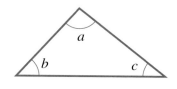

Example 4.3 ▷ Work out the size of the angles marked x and y on the diagram, where y is an exterior angle of the triangle.

The angles in a triangle add up to 180°. Therefore:

$x = 180° - 48° - 110°$

$\quad = 22°$

The angles on a straight line add up to 180°. This gives:

$y = 180° - 22°$

$\quad = 158°$

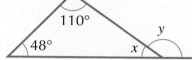

Exercise 4B

1 Calculate the size of the lettered angles in each of these triangles.

a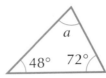

b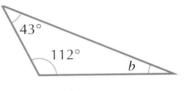

c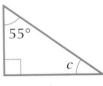

d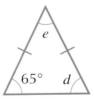

e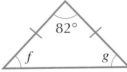

f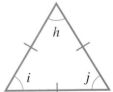

2 Calculate the size of the lettered angles in each of these diagrams. Give an explanation of how you found each angle.

a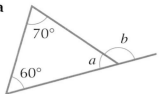

b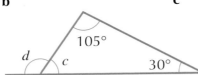

c

d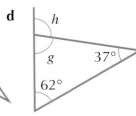

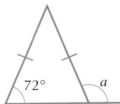 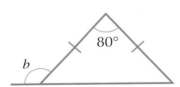 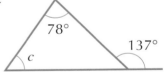

3 Calculate the size of the lettered angle in each of these diagrams. Copy each diagram and show your working to explain how you got each answer.

a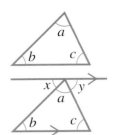

b

c

Extension Work

Example 1

The following two examples show you how to prove geometric statements. Proofs start from basic geometric facts which are known to be true. Algebra is used to combine the basic facts into more complex statements which must be true as well.

Copy these two proofs into your book. Then make sure that you are able to follow each step of each proof.

The sum of the interior angles of a triangle is 180°

To prove $a + b + c = 180°$.

Draw a straight line parallel to one side of the triangle. Let x and y be the other two angles formed on the line with a. This gives:

$x = b$ (alternate angles)
$y = c$ (alternate angles)

The sum of the angles on a straight line is 180°. Therefore:

$a + x + y = 180°$

Substitute $x = b$ and $y = c$, to obtain:

$a + b + c = 180°$

Example 2

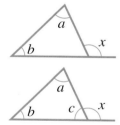

The exterior angle of a triangle is equal to the sum of the two interior opposite angles

To prove $a + b = x$, where x is an exterior angle of the triangle.

Let the other interior angle of the triangle be c.

The sum of the interior angles of a triangle is 180°. Therefore:

$$a + b + c = 180°$$

The sum of the angles on a straight line is 180°. Therefore:

$$x + c = 180°$$

which gives:

$$a + b = x$$

Angles of a quadrilateral

An investigation

Draw a large quadrilateral similar to the one on the right.

Measure each interior angle as accurately as you can, using a protractor. Now add up the four angles. What do you notice?

You should find that your answer is close to 360°.

Now draw a different quadrilateral and find the sum of the angles. How close were you to 360°?

For any quadrilateral, the sum of the interior angles is 360°. So, in the diagram:

$$a + b + c + d = 360°$$

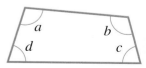

Example 4.4

Work out the sizes of the angles marked p and q on the diagram.

The angles in a quadrilateral add up to 360°, which gives:

$$p = 360° - 135° - 78° - 83°$$
$$= 64°$$

The angles on a straight line add up to 180°, so:

$$q = 180° - 64°$$
$$= 116°$$

Angle q is an **exterior angle** of the quadrilateral.

1. Calculate the size of the lettered angle in each of these quadrilaterals.

a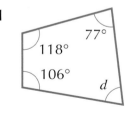

45° 110°
a 75°

b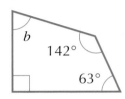

b
142°
63°

c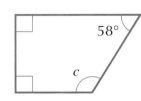

58°
c

d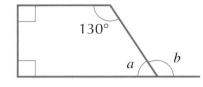

77°
118°
106°
d

e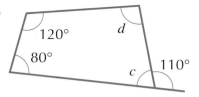

47° *e* 62°
88°

2. Calculate the size of the lettered angles in each of these diagrams. Give an explanation of how you found each angle.

a

130°
a *b*

b

120° *d*
80°
c 110°

3. ABCD is a parallelogram with ∠ADC = 60°.

   a What do you know about a parallelogram?

   b Explain how you could find ∠BAD.

   c Write down the size of ∠ABC and ∠BCD.

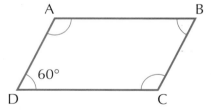

A   B

60°
D   C

4. ABCD is a kite with ∠DAB = 80° and ∠BCD = 50°.

   a Make a sketch of the kite and draw its line of symmetry.

   b What do you know about angles *p* and *q*?

   c Use this information to work out angles *p* and *q*.

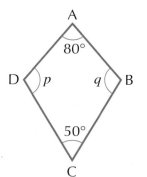

A
80°
D)*p* *q*(B
50°
C

5. PQRS is a trapezium.

   a Work out the size of the angle marked *p*.

   b Write down anything you notice about the angles in the trapezium.

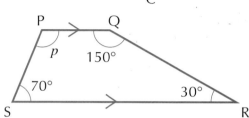

P   Q
p 150°
70°
30°
S   R

1. A quadrilateral can be split into two triangles, as shown in the diagram. Explain how you can use this to show that the sum of the angles in a quadrilateral is 360°.

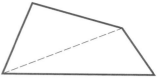

2. a What is the sum of the four angles in the quadrilateral on the right?

   b Write down an equation in terms of x.

   c Solve the equation to find x.

   d Find the size of the four angles in the quadrilateral.

   e What type of quadrilateral is it?

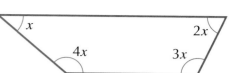

Interior angles of polygons

The angles inside a polygon are known as **interior angles**.

Example 4.5 ▷ Find the sum of the interior angles of a pentagon.

The diagram shows how a pentagon can be split into three triangles from one of its vertices. The sum of the interior angles for each triangle is 180°.

So, the sum of the interior angles of a pentagon is given by:

$$3 \times 180° = 540°$$

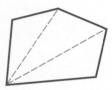

Exercise 4D

1 a Find the sum of the interior angles of **i** a hexagon and **ii** an octagon by splitting each polygon into triangles.

   b Copy and complete the table below. The pentagon has been done for you. You may not need to draw all of the polygons.

Name of polygon	Number of sides	Number of triangles inside polygon	Sum of interior angles
Triangle			
Quadrilateral			
Pentagon	5	3	540°
Hexagon			
Heptagon			
Octagon			

2 Calculate the unknown angle in each of the following polygons.

a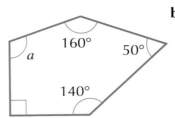

b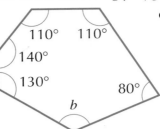

c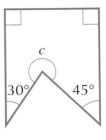

3 a A polygon is regular when all its interior angles are equal and all its sides have the same length.

The shape on the right is a regular pentagon. The sum of its interior angles is 540°. So, the size of each interior angle is 540° ÷ 5 = 108°.

b Copy and complete the table below for regular polygons. The regular pentagon has been done for you.

Regular polygon	Number of sides	Sum of interior angles	Size of each interior angle
Equilateral triangle			
Square			
Regular pentagon	5	540°	108°
Regular hexagon			
Regular octagon			
Regular decagon			

4 Find angle *x* in the pentagon on the right.

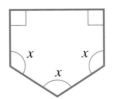

Interior angles in parallel lines

- *a* and *b* are called **interior angles**:

  $a + b = 180°$

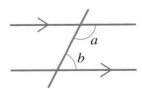

- Calculate x in each of the following diagrams. You may need to set up and solve an equation.

1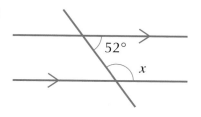

2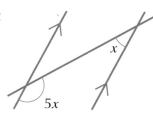

3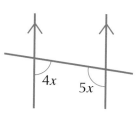

4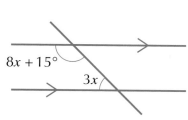

5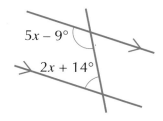

Tessellations and regular polygons

A **tessellation** is a repeating pattern made on a plane (flat) surface with identical shapes which fit together exactly, leaving no gaps.

This section will show you how some of the regular polygons tessellate.

Remember to show how a shape tessellates, draw up to about ten repeating shapes.

Example 4.6 ▷ The diagrams below show how equilateral triangles and squares tessellate.

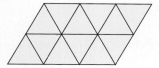 

Exercise 4E

1 On an isometric grid, show how a regular hexagon tessellates.

2 Trace this regular pentagon onto card and cut it out to make a template.

    a Use your template to show that a regular pentagon does not tessellate.

    b Explain why a regular pentagon does not tessellate.

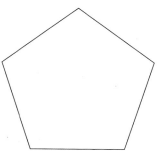

3 Trace this regular octagon onto card and cut it out to make a template.

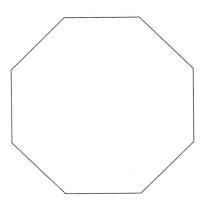

    a Use your template to show that a regular octagon does not tessellate.

    b Explain why a regular octagon does not tessellate.

4 **a** Copy and complete the table below for regular polygons.

Regular polygon	Size of each interior angle	Does this polygon tessellate?
Equilateral triangle		
Square		
Regular pentagon		
Regular hexagon		
Regular octagon		

    b Use the table to explain why only some of the regular polygons tessellate.

    c Do you think that a regular nonagon tessellates? Explain your reasoning.

Extension Work

Polygons can be combined to form a **semi-tessellation**. Two examples are shown below.

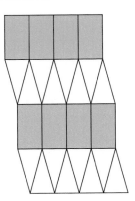

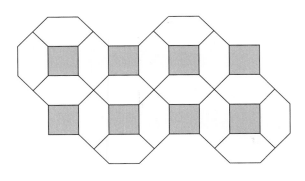

Rectangles and isosceles triangles   **Squares and hexagons**

Invent your own semi-tessellations and make a poster to display in your classroom.

Constructions

Two important geometric constructions are given in Examples 4.7 and 4.8. Carefully work through them yourself. They are important because they produce exact measurements, and are therefore used by architects and in design and technology. You will need a sharp pencil, a straight edge (or ruler), compasses and a protractor. Leave all your construction lines on the diagrams.

Example 4.7

To construct the mid-point and the perpendicular bisector of a line AB

- Draw a line segment AB of any length.
- Set your compasses to any radius greater than half the length of AB.
- Draw two arcs with their centre at A, one above and one below AB.
- With your compasses set at the same radius, draw two arcs with their centre at B, to intersect the first two arcs at C and D.
- Join C and D to intersect AB at X. X is the mid-point of the line AB.
- The line CD is the perpendicular bisector of the line AB.

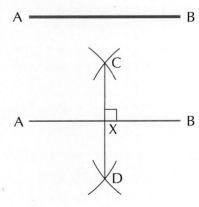

Example 4.8

To construct the bisector of the angle ABC

- Draw an angle ABC of any size.
- Set your compasses to any radius and, with its centre at B, draw an arc to intersect BC at X and AB at Y.
- With your compasses set to any radius, draw two arcs with their centres at X and Y, to intersect at Z.
- Join BZ.
- BZ is the bisector of the angle ABC.
- Then ∠ABZ = ∠CBZ.

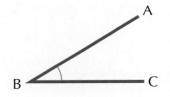

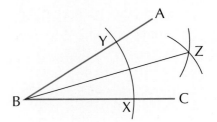

Exercise 4F

1. Use a ruler to draw each of the following lines. Using compasses, construct the perpendicular bisector for each line.

   a 6 cm   **b** 10 cm   **c** 7 cm   **d** 8.4 cm   **e** 5.5 cm

2. Use a protractor to draw each of the following angles. Using compasses, construct the angle bisector for each angle.

   a 40°   **b** 70°   **c** 90°   **d** 55°   **e** 140°

3 The isosceles triangle ABC on the right has a base of 4 cm and a perpendicular height of 5 cm.

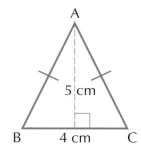

- **a** By constructing the perpendicular bisector of BC, draw an accurate copy of the triangle.

- **b** Measure the length of the sides AB and AC.

Extension Work

1 **To construct an angle of 60°**

Draw a line AB of any length. Set your compasses to a radius of about 4 cm. With its centre at A, draw a large arc to intersect the line at X. Using the same radius and, with its centre at X, draw an arc to intersect the first arc at Y. Join A and Y. Angle YAX is 60°.

Explain how you could use this construction to make angles of 30° and 15°.

2 **To construct the inscribed circle of a triangle**

Draw a triangle ABC with sides of any length. Construct the angle bisectors for each of the three angles. The three angle bisectors will meet at a point O, in the centre of the triangle. Using O as its centre, draw a circle to touch the three sides of the triangle.

The circle is known as the **inscribed circle** of the triangle.

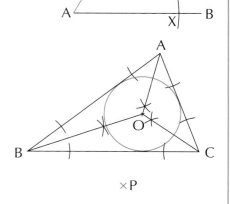

3 **To construct the perpendicular from a point P to a line AB**

Set your compasses to any suitable radius and draw arcs from P to intersect AB at X and Y.

With your compasses set at the same radius, draw arcs with their centres at X and Y, to intersect at Z below AB.

Join PZ. PZ is perpendicular to AB.

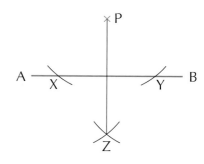

4 **To construct the perpendicular from a point Q on a line XY**

Set your compasses to a radius that is less than half the length of XY. With their centre at Q, draw two arcs on either side of Q to intersect XY at A and B. (You may have to extend the line XY slightly.)

Now set your compasses to a radius that is greater than half the length of XY and, with their centres at A and B, draw arcs above and below XY to intersect at C and D.

Join CD. CD is the perpendicular from the point Q.

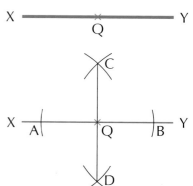

The circle and its parts

A circle is a set of points equidistant from a fixed point, called the **centre**, designated here by O.

You must learn all of the following terms for the different parts of a circle.

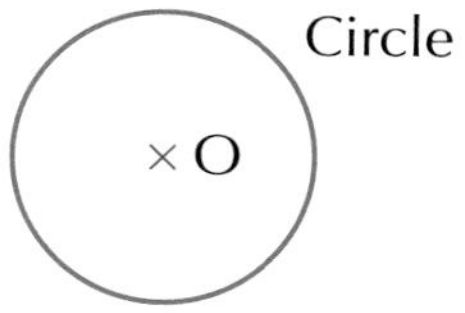

Circle

×O

Circumference The length round a circle. It is a special name for the perimeter of a circle.

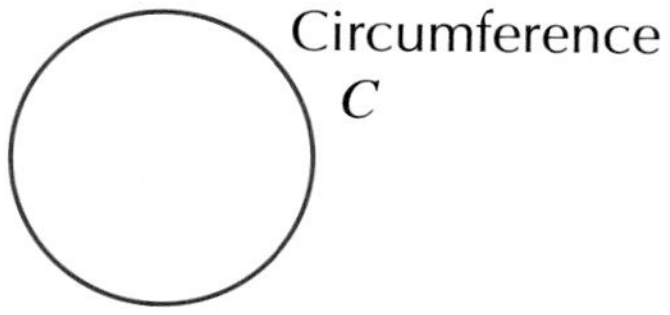

Circumference
C

Arc One of the two parts between two points on a circumference.

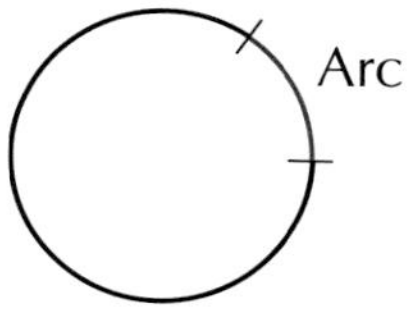

Arc

Radius The distance from the centre of a circle to its circumference. The plural of the term is 'radii'.

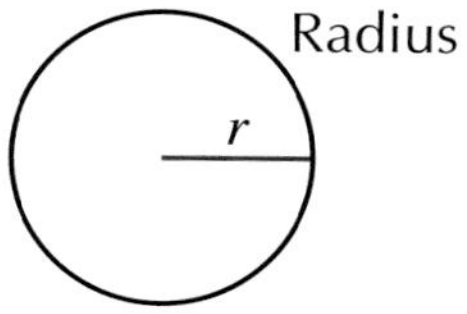

Radius

r

Diameter The distance across a circle through its centre. The diameter d of a circle is twice its radius r, so $d = 2r$.

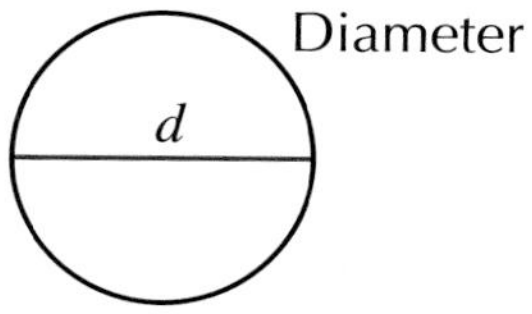

Diameter

d

Chord A straight line which joins two points on the circumference of a circle.

Chord

Tangent A straight line that touches a circle at one point only on its circumference. This point is called the **point of contact**.

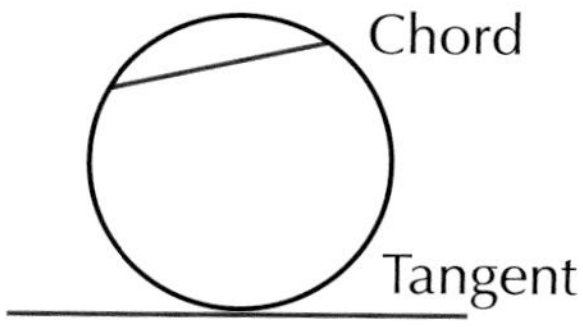

Tangent

Segment The region of a circle enclosed by a chord and an arc. Any chord encloses two segments, which have different areas.

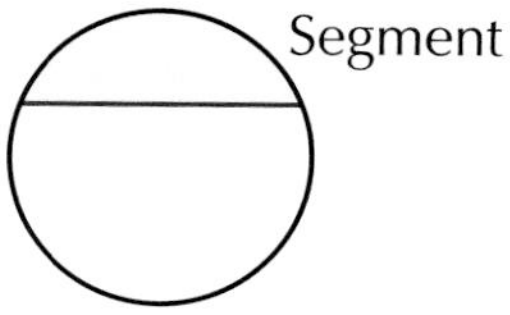

Segment

Sector A portion of a circle enclosed by two radii and one of the arcs between them.

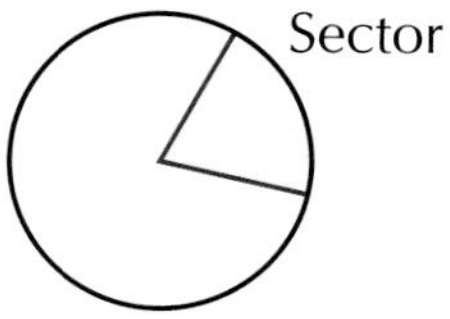

Sector

Semicircle One half of a circle: either of the parts cut off by a diameter.

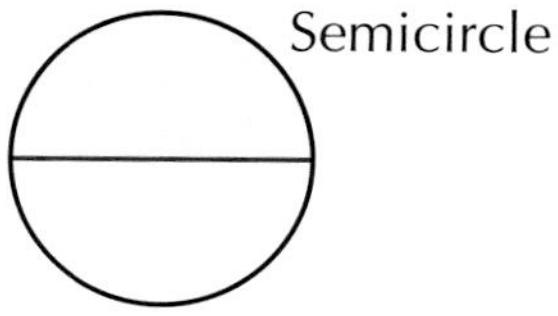

Semicircle

1 Measure the radius of each of the following circles, giving your answer in centimetres. Write down the diameter of each circle.

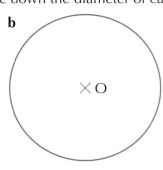

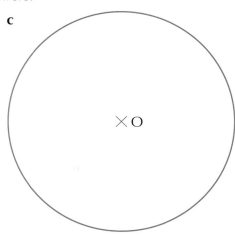

2 Draw circles with the following measurements.

    a Radius = 2.5 cm   **b** Radius = 3.6 cm

    c Diameter = 8 cm   **d** Diameter = 6.8 cm

3 Draw each of the following shapes accurately.

    a   **b**   **c**   **d**

Concentric circles   **Semicircle**   **Quadrant of a circle**   **Sector of a circle**

4 Draw each of the following diagrams accurately.

    a   **b**   **c**

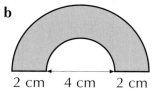

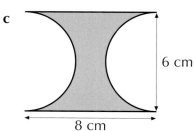

5 Draw a circle with centre O and with a radius of 4 cm. Draw six radii that are 60° apart, as shown in the diagram on the right. Join the points on the circumference to make an inscribed regular hexagon.

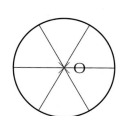

    a Explain why the radii must be 60° apart.

    b Use this method to draw each of these.

        i An inscribed regular pentagon

        ii An inscribed regular octagon

To find the centre of a circle

Draw a circle around a circular object so that the centre is not known.

Draw any two chords on the circle, as shown in the diagram. Then draw the perpendicular bisector for each chord.

The two perpendicular bisectors will intersect at the centre of the circle.

Repeat for circles of various radii.

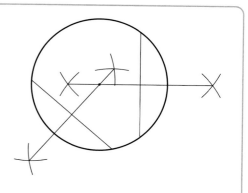

What you need to know for level 4

o Names of the different types of quadrilateral and polygon

What you need to know for level 5

o Interior angles of a triangle add up to 180°

o Interior angles of a quadrilateral add up to 360°

o How to construct the perpendicular bisector of a line and the bisector of an angle

National Curriculum SATs questions

LEVEL 5

1 *1997 Paper 2*

Here is a rough sketch of a sector of a circle.

Make an accurate, full-size drawing of this sector.

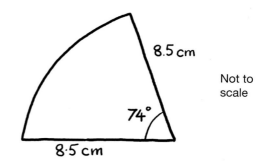

8.5 cm

Not to scale

74°

8·5 cm

2 *2003 Paper 2*

Look at the diagram. Triangle ABD is the reflection of triangle ABC in the line AB.

Copy the statements below and fill in the gaps to explain how to find angle x.

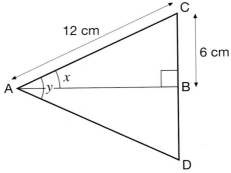

The length of AC is ..12... cm.

The length of AD is ...... cm.

The length of CD is ...... cm.

ACD is an equilateral triangle because ....

so angle y is ......° because ....

so angle x is ......° because ....

CHAPTER 5

Handling Data **1**

<table>
<tr><td>

This chapter is going to show you

- how to construct pie charts
- how to interpret graphs and diagrams
- how to construct and interpret two-way tables
- how to construct and interpret frequency tables

</td><td>

What you should already know

- How to construct ten-sector pie charts
- How to collect data
- How to draw simple frequency diagrams
- How to investigate a statistical problem

</td></tr>
</table>

Pie charts

This section will remind you about ten-sector pie charts, which you looked at in Year 8. It will also show you how to construct pie charts for more complex data.

Example 5.1 ▷ **Ten-sector pie charts**

Draw a pie chart to represent the following set of data, which shows the favourite ice-creams of a group of students.

Ice-cream	Vanilla	Strawberry	Chocolate	Other
Number of students	9	6	12	3

The data adds up to 30 students. Therefore, each sector on the ten-sector pie chart represents 3 students.

So, vanilla gets 3 sectors, strawberry gets 2 sectors, chocolate gets 4 sectors and 'other' gets 1 sector.

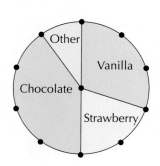

Example 5.2 ▷ **General pie charts**

A travel agent recorded the types of holiday that people booked on one day. Draw a pie chart to represent this information.

Type of holiday	Tour	Flight abroad	Short break	Other
Frequency	18	31	22	19

This time the numbers are more complex. The total number of people is 90.

So, 90 people are represented by the whole pie chart, which contains 360°.

Therefore, one person is represented by 360° ÷ 90 = 4°.

Hence, 18 people are represented by 4° × 18 = 72°.

31 people are represented by 4° × 31 = 124°

22 people are represented by 4° × 22 = 88°

19 people are represented by 4° × 19 = 76°

Now check that the working is correct, adding up these angles. The result should be 360°, which it is!

72° + 124° + 88° + 76° = 360°

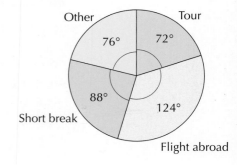

1 Draw pie charts to represent each of the following tables of data.

a The sports chosen by a group of 60 students.

Sport	Football	Netball	Basketball	Fitness
Frequency	17	12	18	13

b The meals taken by 45 teachers.

Meal	School dinner	Packed lunch	Eat out
Frequency	16	23	6

c The favourite music of 36 Year 9 students.

Type of music	Pop	Classical	Rap	Other
Frequency	9	6	8	13

d The ratings of a hotel in a satisfaction survey of 180 customers.

Rating	Excellent	Good	Satisfactory	Poor	Very poor
Frequency	31	82	25	24	18

2 A survey about the cost of visiting a theme park is carried out. The results from 720 visitors are shown in the pie chart.

How many visitors gave each of these replies?

a Expensive

b Quite expensive

c Fair

d Cheap

e Very cheap

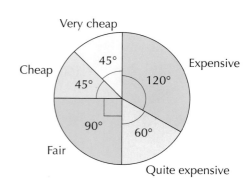

Look again at the sports chosen by a group of 60 students (Question **1**).

Sport	Football	Netball	Basketball	Fitness
Frequency	17	12	18	13

17 out of 60 chose football. Expressing this as a percentage gives:

$\frac{17}{60} \times 100 = 28.3\%$ to 1 dp.

Calculate the percentage of students who chose each of the following.

a   Netball   b   Basketball   c   Fitness

Then find the percentages of each category for each of the other tables in Question 1.

Interpreting graphs and diagrams

In this section you will learn how to **interpret** graphs and diagrams, and how to **criticise** statements made about the data which they contain.

Example 5.3 ▷   The diagram shows how a group of students say they spend their time per week.

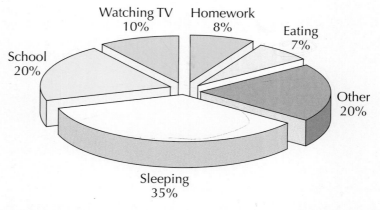

Matt says: 'The diagram shows that students spend too much time at school and doing homework.' Give two arguments to suggest that this is not true.

The diagram represents a group of students, so the data may vary for individual students. It could also be argued, for example, that students spend longer watching TV than doing homework.

1 A journey is shown on the distance–time graph. There are three stages to the journey and two stops.

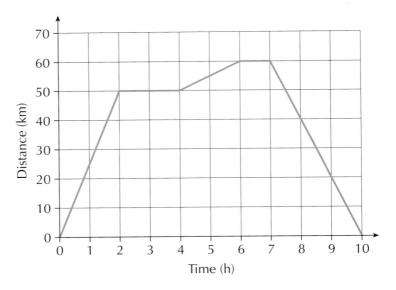

a   How far is travelled in the first stage of the journey?

b   How long is the first stop?

c   Chris says that the total distance travelled is 60 km. Explain why Chris is incorrect.

2 The results of a junior school throwing competition are shown in the bar chart.

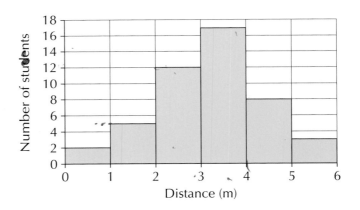

a   How many students threw between 3 and 4 metres?

b   How many students threw between 1 and 2 metres?

c   Alex says: 'The longest throw was 5.4 metres.' Could she be correct? Explain your answer.

d   Becky says: 'The range of the throws is 6 metres.' Explain why she is incorrect.

3 The pie chart shows how crimes were committed in a town over a month.

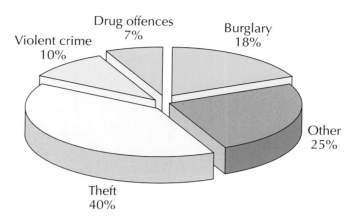

Drug offences 7%

Violent crime 10%

Burglary 18%

Other 25%

Theft 40%

Thirty violent crimes were committed.

a How many drug offences were committed?

b How many offences were committed altogether?

c It is claimed that most crime involves theft. Explain why this is incorrect.

4 The table shows information about the animal populations on four small farms in the years 1995 and 2000.

Farm	Animal population 1995	Animal population 2000
A	143	275
B	284	241
C	86	75
D	102	63
Total	615	654

a Which farm has increased the number of animals between 1995 and 2000?

b Which farm has shown the largest decrease in animal population from 1995 to 2000?

c A newspaper headline says that farm animal populations are increasing. Using the information in the table, criticise this headline.

Extension Work

Find a graph or chart from a newspaper. Write down the facts that the newspaper article is claiming that the graph or chart shows. Use different arguments, referring to the graph or chart, to cast doubt on the facts given.

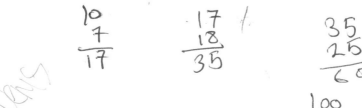

Two-way tables

Jeff and Catherine go to the school car park and record data about the 80 cars parked there. Here is their record.

		Colour of cars				
		Red	White	Blue	Black	Other
Make of cars	Peugeot	8	1	4	1	4
	Ford	11	2	4	2	6
	Vauxhall	5	4	0	0	2
	Citroen	1	2	2	0	3
	Other	6	3	3	4	2

This is called a **two-way table.**

Example 5.4 ▷ Use the two-way table above to answer the questions about the cars in the car park.

  a How many red Fords are there?

  b How many Vauxhalls are not white?

  c How many more blue Peugeots are there than white Citroens?

  a There are 11 red Fords.

  b There are 11 Vauxhalls but 4 are white, so 7 are not white.

  c There are 4 blue Peugeots and 2 white Citroens, so there are 2 more blue Peugeots than white Citroens.

Example 5.5 ▷ An Internet company charges delivery for goods based on the type of delivery – normal delivery (taking 3 to 5 days) or next-day delivery – and also on the cost of the order. The table shows how it is calculated.

Cost of order	Normal delivery (3 to 5 days)	Next-day delivery
£0–£10	£1.95	£4.95
£10.01–£30	£2.95	£4.95
£30.01–£50	£3.95	£6.95
£50.01–£75	£2.95	£4.95
Over £75	Free	£3.00

  a Comment on the difference in delivery charges for normal and next-day delivery.

  b Two items cost £5 and £29. How much would you save by ordering them together **i** using normal delivery and **ii** using next-day delivery?

Example 5.5
continued

a It always costs more using next-day delivery but for goods costing between £10.01 and £30, or between £50.01 and £75, it is only £2 more. It is £3 more for all other orders.

b Using normal delivery and ordering the items separately, it would cost £1.95 + £2.95 = £4.90, but ordering them together would cost £3.95. The saving would be £4.90 − £3.95 = 95p.

Using next-day delivery and ordering the items separately, it would cost £4.95 + £4.95 = £9.90, but ordering them together would cost £6.95. The saving would be £9.90 − £6.95 = £2.95.

Exercise 5C

1 The table shows the number of students who have school lunches in Years 7, 8 and 9.

	Have school lunch	Do not have school lunch
Year 7	120	64
Year 8	97	87
Year 9	80	104

a How does the number of students who have school lunch change as they get older?

b Between which two years are the greatest changes? Explain your answer.

c By looking at the changes in the table, approximately how many students would you expect to not have a school lunch in Year 10?

2 The cost of a set of old toys depends on whether the toys are still in the original boxes and also on the condition of the toys. The table shows the percentage value of a toy compared with its value if it is in perfect condition and boxed.

Condition	Boxed	Not boxed
Excellent	100%	60%
Very good	80%	50%
Good	60%	40%
Average	40%	25%
Poor	20%	10%

a Copy and complete the table.

Condition	Difference between boxed and not boxed
Excellent	100% − 60% = 40%
Very good	
Good	
Average	
Poor	

b Comment on the difference in value between boxed and not boxed as the condition of the toy becomes worse.

3 The table shows the percentage of boys and girls by age group who have mobile phones.

Age	Boys	Girls
10	18%	14%
11	21%	18%
12	42%	39%
13	53%	56%
14	56%	59%
15	62%	64%

   a Work out the differences in the percentages for boys and girls at ages 10 to 15.

   b Write down what you notice about the differences in the percentages for boys and girls.

4 A school analyses the information on the month of birth for 1000 students. The results are shown in the table.

Month	Jan	Feb	Mar	Apr	May	Jun	Jul	Aug	Sep	Oct	Nov	Dec
Boys	34	36	43	39	47	50	44	39	55	53	42	35
Girls	37	31	36	35	44	43	36	40	52	49	43	37

   a On the same grid, plot both sets of values to give a time series graph for the boys and another for the girls.

   b Use the graphs to examine the claim that more children are born in the summer than in the winter.

The heights of 70 Year 9 students are recorded. The results are given in a table (below left) and shown on a frequency diagram (below right).

Height (cm)	Boys	Girls
130–139	3	3
140–149	2	4
150–159	10	12
160–169	14	11
170–179	6	5

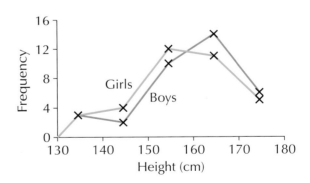

Use the results to examine the claim that boys are taller than girls in Year 9. You may use either the table or the frequency diagram to help you.

Drawing and using frequency diagrams

Look at the picture. How does the shopkeeper know how many clothes of each size he will sell the most of?

Example 5.6

Construct a frequency diagram for the data, given on the right, about the heights of people.

It is important that the diagram has a title and labels as shown.

Height (h) (centimetres)	Frequency
$100 < h \le 120$	9
$120 < h \le 140$	13
$140 < h \le 160$	26
$160 < h \le 180$	15
$180 < h \le 200$	10

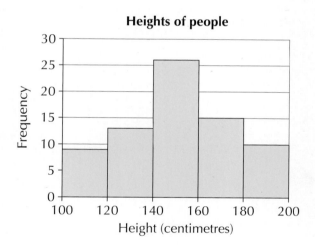

Example 5.7

Construct a frequency diagram to show how lawn-mower sales at a shop vary throughout a year.

Jan	Feb	Mar	Apr	May	Jun	Jul	Aug	Sep	Oct	Nov	Dec
0	25	63	75	92	68	53	32	76	15	0	12

Write down why you think the sales are high in September and why there are some sales in December.

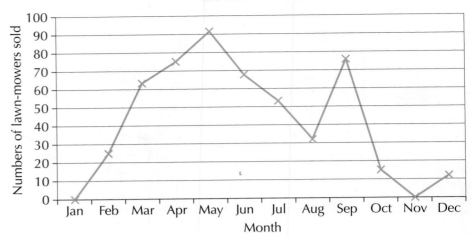

Lawn-mower sales

The reasons for the sales in September could be that the shop reduces the prices in an attempt to sell off stock before winter. The December sales could be Christmas presents.

1 For each frequency table, construct a frequency diagram.

a Time for stoppages added on at the end of 44 football matches.

Time (*t*) minutes	Frequency
$0 < t \leq 1$	3
$1 < t \leq 2$	7
$2 < t \leq 3$	15
$3 < t \leq 4$	12
$4 < t \leq 5$	5
$5 < t \leq 6$	2

b Wages per hour of workers at a factory.

Wages (*W*) £	Frequency
$0 \leq W < 5$	38
$5 \leq W < 10$	20
$10 \leq W < 15$	5
$15 \leq W < 20$	1

c Heights of plants.

Height (*h*) metres	Frequency
$0 < h \leq 0.5$	12
$0.5 < h \leq 1$	19
$1 < h \leq 1.5$	8
$1.5 < h \leq 2$	5
$2 < h \leq 2.5$	3

d Temperatures of coastal towns in Britain on one day in July.

Temperature (T) °C	Frequency
$0 \leq T < 10$	2
$10 \leq T < 20$	16
$20 \leq T < 30$	9
$30 \leq T < 40$	1

2 The following table shows the rainfall, in millimetres, for a town in the north of England.

Month	Jan	Feb	Mar	Apr	May	Jun	Jul	Aug	Sep	Oct	Nov	Dec
Rainfall (mm)	45	36	44	47	51	54	49	55	50	44	51	50

a Construct a line graph of this data.

b Which month had the greatest rainfall?

c Which month had the least rainfall?

d For how many months was the amount of rainfall below 45 mm?

e What is the difference between the amount of rainfall in July and the amount of rainfall in August?

f Between which two consecutive months is there the greatest difference in rainfall?

Extension Work

The table shows population forecasts for the UK and Afghanistan.

Year	2003	2008	2013	2018	2023	2028	2033	2038	2043	2048
Population of UK (millions)	60.1	60.9	61.8	62.7	63.5	64.1	64.5	64.5	64.4	64.1
Population of Afghanistan (millions)	28.7	33.4	36.2	40.1	44.2	48.4	52.7	57.1	61.4	65.6

a Construct a line graph for each country using the same axes.

b Estimate the year when the populations of the two countries will be equal.

c Estimate the year when the population of the UK is at its maximum. State what this maximum population could be.

Statistical investigations

Investigating a problem will involve several steps. An example from PE is given together with an example of how to write a report.

Step	Plan
1 Decide which general topic to study	For this investigation, I am going to find out how to improve students' performance in sport.
2 Specify in more detail	In particular, I am going to investigate the ability of students to throw a cricket ball.
3 Guess what you think could happen. (This is called 'Stating your hypotheses')	I will consider whether a run-up improves performance. I will also compare students of similar heights, as it is possible that height would also affect performance.
4 Conjectures	I think that the distance thrown will improve using a run-up but if the run-up is too long it might then fail to improve performance. I think that Year 11 students of the same height may be physically stronger and would therefore throw further.
5 Sources of information required	I will carry out a survey of the distance thrown with different lengths of run-up.
6 Relevant data	I am going to choose students from Year 9 and Year 11, arranged in three groups according to height: short, medium height and tall. I will use 5 boys and 5 girls in each group. I will try to use students of different sporting abilities. Each student will have 3 throws, one with no run-up, one with a 5 metre run-up and one with a 10 metre run-up.
7 Possible problems	I will allow each student the same length of time, 5 minutes, to warm up. I will organise the event so that the throws are always taken in the same order. For example, the first throw for every student has no run-up. This should produce more reliable results.
8 Possible problems	I will put each student into a category according to their height and Year group. I will then record the distance for each throw.
9 Decide on appropriate level of accuracy	I will round off all measurements to the nearest 10 cm.
10 Determine sample size	In order to collect all this information effectively, I will ask a group of friends to help me.
11 Construct tables for large sets of raw data in order to make work manageable	I will create a two-way table to record my results for each group.
12 Decide which statistic is most suitable	I will calculate the mean for each group of results and then compare its value with my predictions.

Here is an example of a recording sheet for Year 9 students of medium height.

Year 9 Medium height	Student 1	Student 2	Student 3	Student 4	Student 5
No run-up					
5 m run-up					
10 m run-up					

Exercise 5E

1 List in order the missing words in each plan given below.

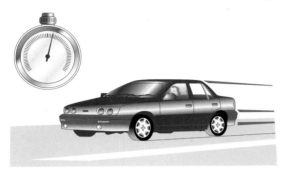

Missing words for Science Plan are:

car	bias	not	books
petrol	nearest	investigate	engine

Missing words for Geography Plan are:

mean	incomes	information	compare
sample	average	Internet	housing

	Step	Q1 Science Plan	Q2 Geography Plan
1	Decide which general topic to study	I am going to …… the effect of engine size on a car's acceleration.	I am going to …… life expectancy against the cost of housing.
2	Specify in more detail	I will begin by studying only one make of ……. .	I will compare house prices in Yorkshire with those in the South-East.
3	Guess what you think could happen. (This is called 'Stating your hypotheses')	I am going to try to find out if a bigger …… always means that a car can accelerate faster.	I am going to investigate whether people in expensive …… tend to live longer.
4	Conjectures	It may be that more powerful engines tend to be in heavier cars and therefore the acceleration is …… affected. I am sure that larger engines in the same model of car will improve acceleration.	As people in expensive housing have greater …… , they may also have a longer life expectancy.
5	Sources of information required	I am going to use car magazines and …… to find information on engine sizes and the acceleration times for 0–60 mph.	I am going to use the library and search the …… for census data for each area.

Step	Q1 Science Plan	Q2 Geography Plan
6 Relevant data	I am using 0–60 mph because the government requires car manufacturers to publish the time taken to accelerate from 0–60 mph.	I will record the …… cost of housing for each area and also the life expectancy for each area.
7 Possible problems	I will keep a record of the make of car, the engine size and the acceleration time. I will only compare petrol engines with other …… engines and not with diesel engines to avoid …… in my results.	
8 Possible problems	I will also find out and record the weight of each car, as this is part of my guess at what will affect the results.	When I find the …… that I need, I will make a note of where it came from.
9 Decide on appropriate level of accuracy	I will round engine sizes to the …… 100 cm^3. For example, a car with an engine capacity of 1905 cc (this is the same as cm^3 but is what the motor trade use) will be recorded as 1900 cc.	
10 Determine sample size		
11 Construct tables for large sets of raw data in order to make work manageable		I will group the data about the population in age groups of 5-year intervals.
12 Decide which statistic is most suitable		I will make sure that I look at at least 30 pieces of data for each area so that my …… is large enough to calculate the …… and have a reliable answer.

Extension Work

Think of a problem related to students who cycle to school. Collect as much data as you can, and write up your plan.

Use the planning steps on page 82 as your guides.

What you need to know for level 4

- How to group data in equal class intervals
- How to represent collected data in frequency diagrams
- How to interpret frequency diagrams
- How to present information in a clear and organised way

What you need to know for level 5

- How to interpret graphs and diagrams, including pie charts
- How to draw conclusions from graphs and diagrams
- How to identify and obtain necessary information

National Curriculum SATs questions

LEVEL 4

1 *1997 Paper 2*

There are 50 children altogether in a playgroup.

a How many of the children are girls? What percentage of the children are girls?

b 25 of the children are 4 years old.
20 of the children are 3 years old.
5 of the children are 2 years old.

Show this information on a copy of the diagram on the right.

Label each part clearly.

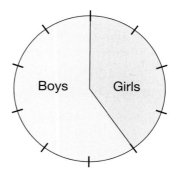

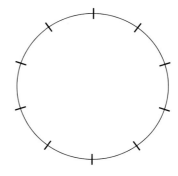

2 *1999 Paper 2*

The graph shows the average heights of young children.

a What is the average height of girls aged 30 months?

b What is the average height of boys aged 36 months?

c Jane is average height for her age. Her height is 80 cm.

Use the graph to find Jane's age.

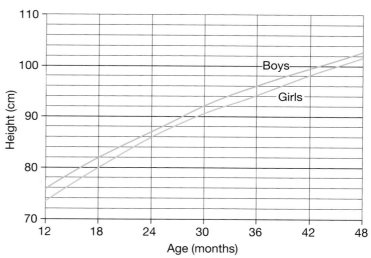

d The table shows approximately how much an average girl grows each year between the ages of 12 and 48 months. Use the graph to complete the table.

Age (months)	Approximate height at start (cm)	Approximate height at end (cm)	Approximate growth (cm)
12 to 24	74	86	12
24 to 36	86		
36 to 48			

e This formula tells you how tall a boy is likely to be when he grows up.

> Add the mother's and father's heights.
> Divide by 2.
> Add 7 cm to the result.
> The boy is likely to be this height, plus or minus 10 cm.

Marc's mother is 168 cm tall. His father is 194 cm tall.

What is the greatest height Marc is likely to be when he grows up?

Show your working.

LEVEL 5

3 *1997 Paper 2*

The Highway Code states the minimum distance there should be between cars. There are different distances for bad weather and good weather.

The graph on the right shows this.

a The weather is bad. A car is travelling at 40 miles per hour.

What is the minimum distance it should be from the car in front?

b The weather is good. A car is travelling at 55 miles per hour.

What is the minimum distance it should be from the car in front?

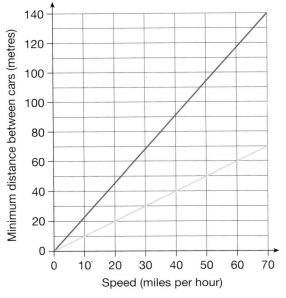

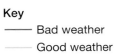

Key
——— Bad weather
——— Good weather

4 *2000 Paper 1*

Maria and Kay ran a 1500 metres race. The distance–time graph on the right shows the race.

Use the graph to help you fill in the gaps in this report of the race.

> Just after the start of the race, Maria was in the lead. At 600 metres, Maria and Kay were level. Then Kay was in the lead for …… minutes. At …… metres, Maria and Kay were level again.
>
> …… won the race. Her total time was …… minutes. …… finished …… minutes later.

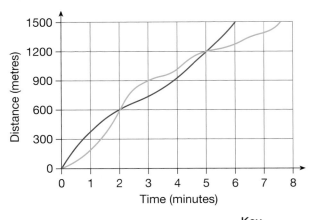

Key
——— Maria
——— Kay

CHAPTER 6

Shape, Space and Measures 2

This chapter is going to show you

- how to calculate the area of a triangle, a parallelogram and a trapezium
- how to calculate the area of a compound shape
- how to calculate the volume of a cuboid
- how to convert imperial units to metric units
- how to find the mid-point of a line segment

What you should already know

- How to find the area of a rectangle
- How to calculate the surface area of a cuboid
- How to convert one metric unit to another
- How to plot points in all four quadrants

Area of a triangle

To find the area, A, of a triangle, you need to know the length of its base, b, and its height, h. The height of the triangle is sometimes known as its **perpendicular height**.

The diagram shows that the area of the triangle is half of the area of a rectangle, the length of whose sides are b and h:

Area 1 = Area 2

and

Area 3 = Area 4

So, the area of a triangle is $\frac{1}{2} \times$ base $\times$ height. That is:

$$A = \tfrac{1}{2} \times b \times h = \tfrac{1}{2}bh = \frac{b \times h}{2}$$

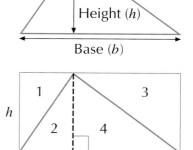

Remember that the metric units of area in common use are:

- Square millimetre (mm²)
- Square centimetre (cm²)
- Square metre (m²)

Example 6.1 ▷ Find the area of the right-angled triangle shown on the right.

$$A = \frac{6 \times 4}{2} = \frac{24}{2} = 12 \text{ cm}^2$$

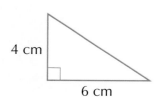

4 cm

6 cm

Example 6.2 Find the area of the triangle shown on the right.

$$A = \frac{8 \times 5}{2} = \frac{40}{2} = 20 \text{ cm}^2$$

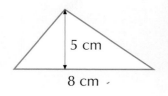

To find the area of a compound shape, first see whether it can be broken down into rectangles and triangles. Next, find the area of each rectangle and triangle separately. Then add together all the areas to obtain the total area of the shape.

Example 6.3 Calculate the area of this shape:

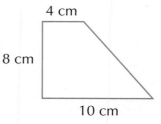

Divide the shape into a rectangle A and a triangle B.

Area of A = 8 × 4 = 32 cm²

Area of B = $\frac{6 \times 8}{2} = \frac{48}{2} = 24$ cm²

Area of shape = 32 + 24 = 56 cm²

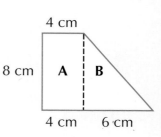

Exercise 6A

1 Find the area of each of the following right-angled triangles.

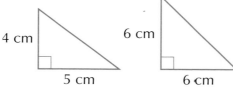
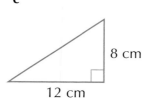
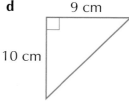

2 Find the area of each of the following triangles.

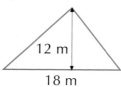

3 Copy and complete the table for triangles **a** to **d**.

Triangle	Base	Height	Area
a	3 cm	4 cm	
b	5 cm	3 cm	
c	4 cm		12 cm²
d		8 cm	20 cm²

4 Find the area of each of the right-angled triangles drawn on the centimetre-square grid below.

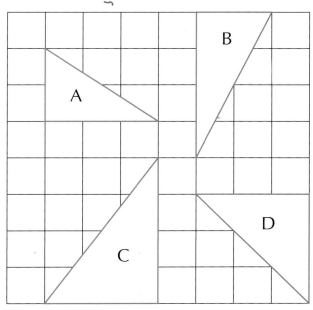

5 Find the area of each compound shape below.

a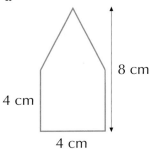

b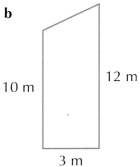

c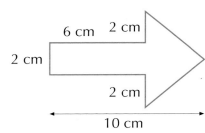

6 The diagram on the right is a plan of a garden.

    a   Find the area of the flower bed.

    b   Hence find the area of the lawn.

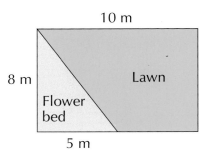

Extension Work

The right-angled triangle shown has an area of 24 cm².

Find other right-angled triangles, with different measurements, which also have an area of 24 cm².

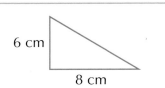

Area of a parallelogram

To find the area, A, of a parallelogram, you need to know the length of its base, b, and its height, h. The height of the parallelogram is sometimes known as its **perpendicular height**.

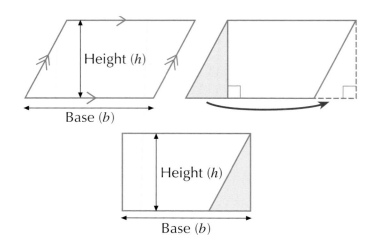

The diagrams show that the parallelogram has the same area as that of a rectangle with the same base and height. So, the area of a parallelogram is base × height. That is:

$$A = b \times h = bh$$

Example 6.4 ▶ Calculate the area of this parallelogram.

Here, $b = 10$ cm and $h = 6$ cm, which gives:
$$A = 6 \times 10 = 60 \text{ cm}^2$$

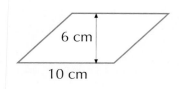

Area of a trapezium

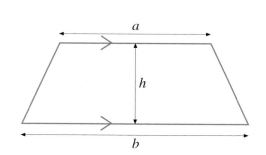

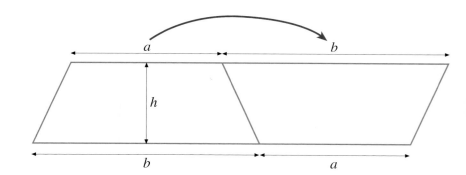

To find the area of a trapezium, you need to know the length of its two parallel sides, a and b, and the perpendicular height, h, between the parallel sides.

The diagram shows how two equivalent trapezia fit together to form a parallelogram. So, the area of a trapezium is $\frac{1}{2} \times$ the sum of the lengths of its parallel sides × its height. That is:

$$A = \tfrac{1}{2} \times (a + b) \times h = \tfrac{1}{2}(a + b)h$$
$$= \frac{(a + b)h}{2}$$

Example 6.5 ▷   Calculate the area of this trapezium.

Here, $a = 5$ cm, $b = 9$ cm and $h = 4$ cm, which gives:

$$A = \tfrac{1}{2} \times (9 + 5) \times 4$$
$$= \frac{14 \times \cancel{4}^2}{\cancel{2}}$$
$$= 28 \text{ cm}^2$$

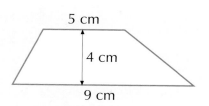

Exercise 6B

1 Find the area of each of the following parallelograms.

a

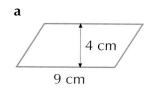

4 cm
9 cm

b

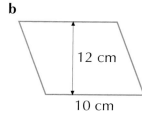

12 cm
10 cm

c

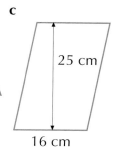

25 cm
16 cm

d

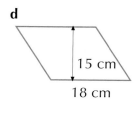

15 cm
18 cm

2 Find the area of each of the following parallelograms.

a

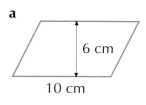

6 cm
10 cm

b

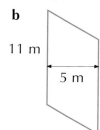

11 m
5 m

c

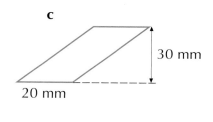

30 mm
20 mm

3 Copy and complete the table below for parallelograms **a** to **d**.

Parallelogram	Base	Height	Area
a	5 cm	6 cm	
b	8 cm	10 cm	
c	4 cm		8 cm²
d		5 cm	100 cm²

4 The area of the parallelogram is 27 cm². Find the perpendicular height, h, of the parallelogram.

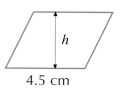

h
4.5 cm

5 Find the area of each of the following trapezia.

a

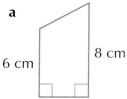

6 cm
8 cm
4 cm

b

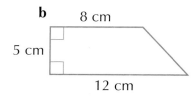

8 cm
5 cm
12 cm

c

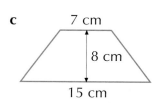

7 cm
8 cm
15 cm

6 Copy and complete the table below for trapezia **a** to **d**.

Trapezium	Length a	Length b	Height h	Area A
a	5 cm	7 cm	4 cm	
b	8 cm	2 cm	5 cm	
c	4 m	2 m	1 m	
d	5 m	4 m	2 m	

7 The side of a swimming pool is a trapezium, as shown in the diagram below. Calculate its area.

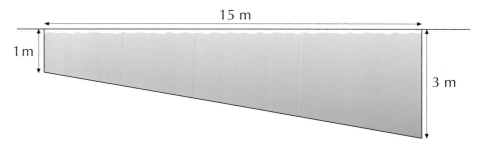

Extension Work

1 The diagram shows the measurements of a sauce bottle label. Calculate its area.

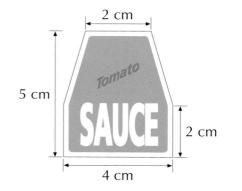

2 Find the solid area of this mathematical stencil, which has the shapes cut out.

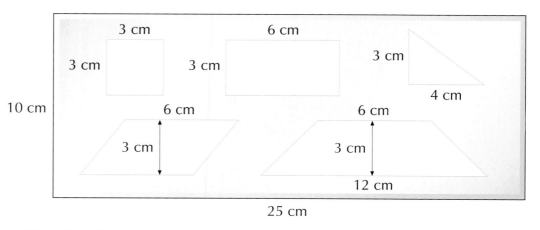

Volume of a cuboid

Volume is the amount of space inside a three-dimensional (3-D) shape.

The diagram shows a cuboid which measures 4 cm by 3 cm by 2 cm. The cuboid is made up of cubes of edge length 1 cm. The top layer consists of 12 cubes and, since there are two layers, the cuboid has altogether 24 cubes.

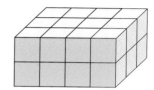

The volume of the cuboid is therefore found by calculating:

$$4 \text{ cm} \times 3 \text{ cm} \times 2 \text{ cm} = 24 \text{ cm}^3.$$

Hence, the volume of a cuboid is found by multiplying its length by its width by its height:

Volume of cuboid = length × width × height

$$V = l \times w \times h = lwh$$

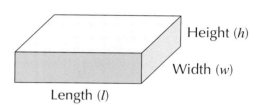

Height (*h*)

Width (*w*)

Length (*l*)

The metric units of volume in common use are:
- Cubic millimetre (mm^3)
- Cubic centimetre (cm^3)
- Cubic metre (m^3)

The **capacity** of a 3-D shape is the volume of liquid or gas it can hold. The metric unit of capacity is the litre (l), where:
- 1 litre = 1000 cm^3
- 1000 litres = 1 m^3

Example 6.6

Find the volume of the cuboid shown on the right.

The volume of the cuboid is given by:

$$V = lwh$$

Putting in the values for *l*, *w* and *h* gives:

$$V = 5 \times 4 \times 3$$
$$= 60 \text{ cm}^3$$

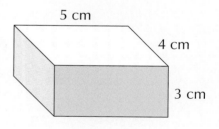

5 cm

4 cm

3 cm

Example 6.7 ▷

Calculate the volume of the tank shown. Then work out the capacity of the tank in litres.

$$V = lwh$$

Putting in the values for *l*, *w* and *h* gives:

$$V = 50 \times 30 \times 10 = 15\,000 \text{ cm}^3$$

Since 1000 cm^3 = 1 litre, the capacity of the tank = 15 000 ÷ 1000 = 15 litres.

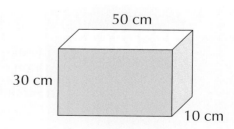

50 cm

30 cm

10 cm

1 Find the volume of each of the following cuboids.

a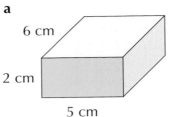

6 cm

2 cm

5 cm

b

8 cm

6 cm

10 cm

c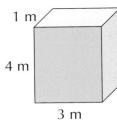

1 m

4 m

3 m

2 Find the capacity, in litres, of each of the following cuboid containers.

a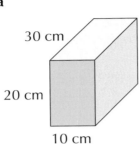

30 cm

20 cm

10 cm

b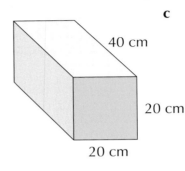

40 cm

20 cm

20 cm

c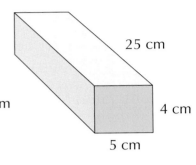

25 cm

4 cm

5 cm

3 Copy and complete the table below for cuboids **a** to **d**.

Cuboid	Length l	Width w	Height h	Volume V
a	5 cm	3 cm	2 cm	
b	6 cm	4 cm	3 cm	
c	3 m	2 m	1 m	
d	5 m	4 m		60 m³

4 Find the volume for each of the cubes with the following edge lengths.

a   2 cm   b   5 cm   c   10 cm

5 Find the volume of a hall that is 30 m long, 15 m wide and 8 m high.

6 The diagram shows the dimensions of a swimming pool.

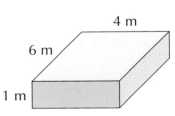

a   Find the volume of the pool, giving your answer in cubic metres.

b   How many litres of water does the pool hold when it is full?

4 m

6 m

1 m

7 The diagram shows the dimensions of a rectangular carton of orange juice.

a   Find the volume of the carton, giving your answer in cubic centimetres.

b   How many litres of orange juice does the carton hold?

12 cm

5 cm

Orange Juice

25 cm

1 The diagrams below show three different packaging boxes.

25 cm

20 cm

5 cm

£1.25

CORN FLAKES

TEA BAGS

240

8 cm

20 cm

16 cm

tissues

5 cm

30 cm

15 cm

a Which box has the greatest volume?

b Which box has the greatest total surface area?

2 Calculate the volume of each of the following 3-D shapes.

a

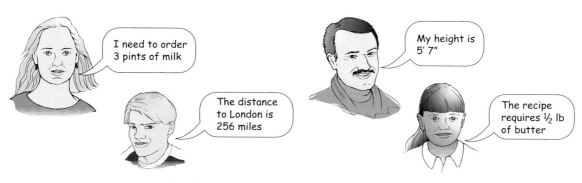

3 m

1 m

1 m

2 m

5 m

b

30 m

36 m

8 m

12 m

60 m

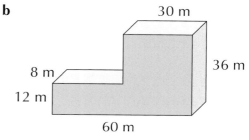

Imperial units

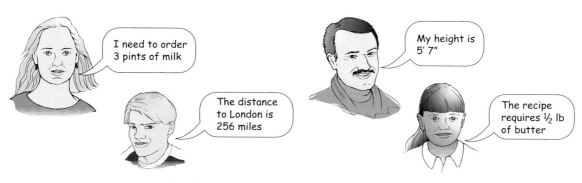

I need to order 3 pints of milk

The distance to London is 256 miles

My height is 5' 7"

The recipe requires ½ lb of butter

In Britain, there is a gradual switch to the metric system of units. But many people still prefer to use the imperial system of units, as the examples on the left show.

The following imperial units are still commonly used, so you should be familiar with them.

Imperial units of length

12 inches (in) = 1 foot (ft)
3 feet = 1 yard (yd)
1760 yards = 1 mile

Imperial units of mass

16 ounces (oz) = 1 pound (lb)
14 pounds = 1 stone (st)
2240 pounds = 1 ton

Imperial units of capacity

8 pints (pt) = 1 gallon (gal)

Example 6.8 Change 3 ft 6 in into inches.

1 ft = 12 in, so 3 ft = 3 × 12 = 36 in

Hence, 3 ft 6 in = 36 + 6 = 42 in

Example 6.9 Change 32 lb into stones and pounds.

1 st = 14 lb, so divide 32 lb by 14, which gives 2 stones with 4 pounds left over.

Hence, 32 lb = 2 st 4 lb

(Note that if you use a calculator, the answer will be given as a decimal number.)

Rough metric equivalents of imperial units

As Britain changes to the metric system, you need to be able to convert from imperial units to metric units by using suitable approximations. It is useful to know the following rough metric equivalents of imperial units. If accuracy is required, the exact conversion factor should be used. The symbol ≈ means 'is approximately equal to'.

Units of length	Units of mass	Units of capacity
1 in ≈ 2.5 cm	1 oz ≈ 30 g	$1\frac{3}{4}$ pints ≈ 1 l
1 yard ≈ 1 metre	1 lb ≈ 500 g	1 gallon ≈ 4.5 l
5 miles ≈ 8 km		

Example 6.10 Approximately how many kilometres are in 20 miles?

5 miles ≈ 8 km

So, 20 miles ≈ 4 × 8 ≈ 32 km

Example 6.11 Approximately how many gallons are in 18 litres?

1 gallon ≈ 4.5 litres

So, divide 18 litres by 4.5, which gives 4 gallons.

Exercise 6D

1 Change each of the following into the unit given in brackets.

a 4 ft (in)	**b** 2 ft 8 in (in)	**c** 4 yd (ft)	**d** 10 yd (ft)
e 2 miles (yd)	**f** 2 lb (oz)	**g** 1 lb 4 oz (oz)	**h** 5 st (lb)
i 2 st 10 lb (lb)	**j** 5 gallons (pints)	**k** $3\frac{1}{2}$ gallons (pints)	**l** 4 yd 2 ft (ft)
m $2\frac{1}{2}$ miles (yd)	**n** 2 yd 1 ft (in)		

2 Change each of the following into the units given in brackets.

a 24 in (ft)	**b** 40 in (ft and in)	**c** 15 ft (yd)
d 20 ft (yd and ft)	**e** 48 oz (lb)	**f** 8 oz (lb)
g 35 oz (lb and oz)	**h** 56 lb (st)	**i** 40 lb (st and lb)
j 16 pints (gallons)	**k** 25 pints (gallons and pints)	

3 Change each of the following imperial quantities into the approximate metric quantity given in brackets.

    a 3 in (cm)   **b** 12 in (cm)   **c** 12 ft (m)   **d** 30 ft (m)

    e 10 miles (km)   **f** 25 miles (km)   **g** 2 oz (g)   **h** 5 oz (g)

    i 2 lb (g)   **j** 7 pints (l)   **k** 10 gallons (l)

4 Pierre is on holiday in England and he sees this sign near to his hotel. Approximately how many metres is it from his hotel to the beach?

5 Mike is travelling on a German autobahn and he sees this road sign. He knows that it means that the speed limit is 120 kilometres per hour. What is the approximate speed limit in miles per hour?

6 Steve needs 6 gallons of petrol to fill the tank of his car. The pump dispenses petrol only in litres. Approximately how many litres of petrol does he need?

7 A newborn baby weighs 8 lb. What is the approximate weight of the baby in kilograms?

8 The length of a cricket pitch is 22 yards. What is the approximate length of the pitch in metres?

Extension Work

  1   Working in pairs or groups, draw a table to show each person's height and weight in imperial and in metric units.

  2 **a** Calculate the number of inches in a mile.

       b Calculate the number of ounces in a ton.

Finding the mid-point of a line segment

The next example will remind you how to plot points in all four quadrants using *x*- and *y*- coordinates.

It will also show you how to find the coordinates of the mid-point of a line which joins two points.

Example 6.12

The coordinates of the points of A, B, C and D on the grid are A(4, 4), B(–2, 4), C(2, 1) and D(2, –3).

The mid-point of the line segment which joins A to B is X. (X is usually referred to as the mid-point of AB.) From the diagram, the coordinates of X are (1, 4). Notice that the y-coordinates are the same for all three points on the line.

The mid-point of CD is Y. From the diagram, the coordinates of Y are (2, –1). Notice that the x-coordinates are the same for all three points on the line.

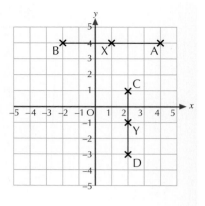

1 Copy the grid on the right on to centimetre-square paper. Then plot the points A, B, C, D, E and F.

    a Write down the coordinates of the points A, B, C, D, E and F.

    b Using the grid to help you, write down the coordinates of the mid-point of each of the following line segments:

       i AB   **ii** AC   **iii** BD

       iv CE   **v** DF

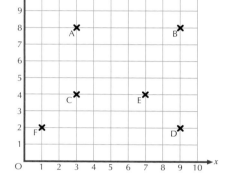

2 Copy the grid on the right on to centimetre-square paper and plot the points J, K, L and M.

    a Write down the coordinates of the points J, K, L and M.

    b Join the points to form the trapezium JKLM. Using the grid to help you, write down the coordinates of the mid-point of each of the following line segments:

       i JK   **ii** JM   **iii** LM   **iv** KL

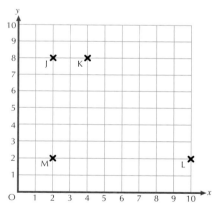

3 Copy the grid on the right and plot the points A, B, C, D, E and F.

    a Write down the coordinates of the points A, B, C, D, E and F.

    b Using the grid to help, write down the coordinates of the mid-point of each of the following line segments:

       i AB   **ii** CD   **iii** BE   **iv** EF

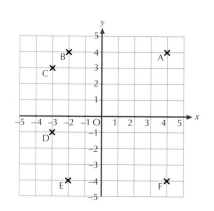

4 Copy the grid on the right and plot the points P, Q, R and S.

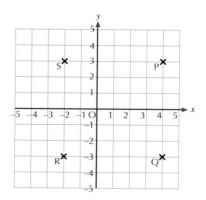

    a Write down the coordinates of the points P, Q, R and S.

    b Join the points to form the rectangle PQRS. Using the grid to help, write down the coordinates of the mid-point of each of the following lines:

        i PQ   **ii** QR   **iii** PS   **iv** SR

    c Write down the coordinates of the mid-point of the diagonal PR.

Extension Work

1   **a** Copy and complete the table below, using the points on the grid to the right. The first row of the table has been completed for you.

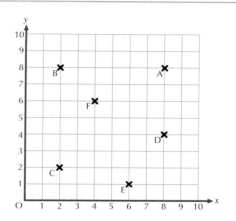

Line segment	Coordinates of first point on line segment	Coordinates of second point on line segment	Coordinates of mid-point of line segment
AB	A(8, 8)	B(2, 8)	(5, 8)
AD			
BC			
BF			
AF			
CE			

    b Can you spot a connection between the coordinates of the first and second points and the coordinates of the mid-point? Write down a rule in your own words.

2 By using the rule you found in Question **1** or by plotting the points on a coordinate grid, find the mid-points of the line which joins each of the following pairs of coordinate points.

    a A(3, 2) and B(3, 6)   **b** C(4, 6) and D(6, 10)

    c E(3, 2) and F(5, 4)   **d** G(8, 6) and H(2, 3)

    e I(5, 6) and J(–3 , –2)

National Curriculum SATs questions

LEVEL 5

1 *2000 Paper 2*

How many kilometres are there in 5 miles?

Copy and complete the missing part of the sign.

2 *2002 Paper 1*

A scale measures in grams and in ounces.

Use the scale to answer these questions.

a About how many ounces is 400 grams?

b About how many grams is 8 ounces?

c About how many ounces is 1 kilogram?
Explain your answer.

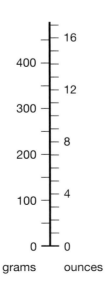

3   *2003 Paper 2*

In this question, the grids are centimetre-square grids.

a   Draw a rectangle that has an area of 12 cm².

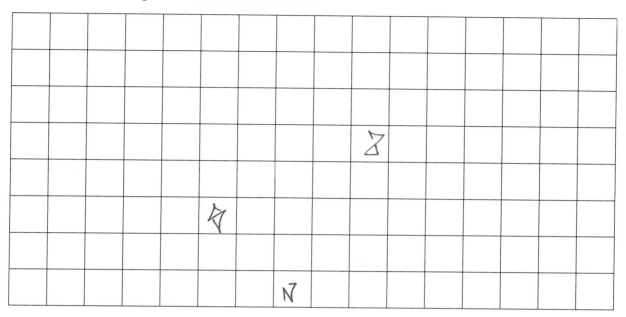

b   Draw a triangle that has an area of 6 cm².

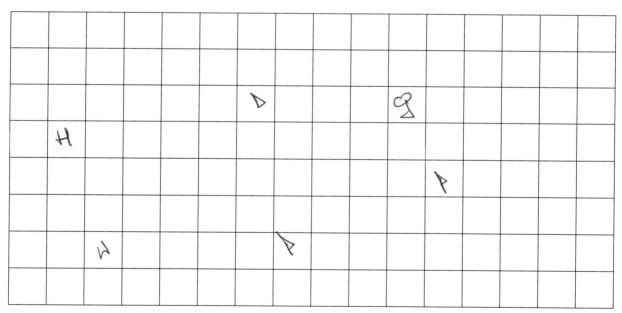

This chapter is going to show you

- how to extend your ability to work with powers of 10
- how to round numbers and use rounded numbers to estimate the results of calculations
- how to write recurring decimals
- how to multiply and divide decimals
- how to use your calculator efficiently

What you should already know

- How to multiply and divide by 10 and 100
- Basic column methods for addition, subtraction, multiplication and division

Powers of 10

You have met powers of 10 before. This section will remind you how to use them to solve problems. The following table shows you some powers of 10.

Power	10^0	10^1	10^2	10^3	10^4
Value	1	10	100	1000	10 000

Example 7.1

Multiply and divide each of the following numbers by **i** 10^2 and **ii** 10^3.

a 0.752 **b** 1.508 **c** 0.0371

You have $10^2 = 100$ and $10^3 = 1000$. Hence, multiplying and dividing by each of them gives:

a **i** $0.752 \times 10^2 = 75.2$; $0.752 \div 10^2 = 0.007\,52$
    ii $0.752 \times 10^3 = 752$; $0.752 \div 10^3 = 0.000\,752$

b **i** $1.508 \times 10^2 = 150.8$; $1.508 \div 10^2 = 0.015\,08$
    ii $1.508 \times 10^3 = 1508$; $1.508 \div 10^3 = 0.001\,508$

c **i** $0.0371 \times 10^2 = 3.71$; $0.0371 \div 10^2 = 0.000\,371$
    ii $0.0371 \times 10^3 = 37.1$; $0.0371 \div 10^3 = 0.000\,0371$

Example 7.2

Multiply and divide each of the following numbers by **i** 0.1 and **ii** 0.01.

a 3.45 **b** 0.089 **c** 7632

Multiplying and dividing by each of them gives:

a **i** $3.45 \times 0.1 = 0.345$; $3.45 \div 0.1 = 34.5$
    ii $3.45 \times 0.01 = 0.0345$; $3.45 \div 0.01 = 345$

b **i** $0.089 \times 0.1 = 0.0089$; $0.089 \div 0.1 = 0.89$
    ii $0.089 \times 0.01 = 0.000\,89$; $0.089 \div 0.01 = 8.9$

c **i** $7632 \times 0.1 = 763.2$; $7632 \div 0.1 = 76\,320$
    ii $7632 \times 0.01 = 76.32$; $7632 \div 0.01 = 763\,200$

1 Multiply each of the following numbers by **i** 10 and **ii** 10^2.

    a 8.7   **b** 0.32   **c** 103.5   **d** 0.09   **e** 23.06

2 Divide each of the following numbers by **i** 10 and **ii** 10^2.

    a 8.7   **b** 0.32   **c** 103.5   **d** 0.09   **e** 23.06

3 Divide each of the following numbers by **i** 0.1 and **ii** 0.01.

    a 2.7   **b** 0.45   **c** 207   **d** 0.08   **e** 41.7

4 Multiply each of the following numbers by **i** 0.1 and **ii** 0.01.

    a 2.7   **b** 0.45   **c** 207   **d** 0.08   **e** 41.7

5 Calculate each of these.

a 6.34×100	**b** $47.3 \div 100$	**c** 66×1000	**d** $2.7 \div 1000$
e $3076 \times 10\,000$	**f** $7193 \div 10\,000$	**g** 9.2×0.1	**h** $0.64 \div 0.1$
i 0.84×0.01	**j** $8.71 \div 0.01$	**k** 3.76×100	**l** $2.3 \div 100$
m 0.09×100	**n** $3.09 \div 10$	**o** 2.35×10	**p** $0.01 \div 100$

6 Work out each of the following. Remember that $10^2 = 100$ and $10^3 = 1000$.

a 39×10^2	**b** $48 \div 10^2$	**c** 5.8×10^3	**d** $3.4 \div 10^2$
e 5.61×10^3	**f** $0.48 \div 10^2$	**g** 0.328×10^3	**h** $0.032 \div 10^2$
i $467 \div 10^2$	**j** 3208×10^2	**k** $234.1 \div 10^3$	**l** 0.009×10^3

Extension Work

Calculators sometimes display numbers in this way. Called standard form, it is usually used to write very large or very small numbers in a compact way.

The power shown is a power of 10. Writing out the number in full gives:.

$7.3^{02} = 7.3 \times 10^2 = 7.3 \times 100 = 730$

$5.4^{03} = 5.4 \times 10^3 = 5.4 \times 1000 = 5400$

Work out the number shown by each of these calculator displays.

    a 8.8^{02} **b** 5.32^{04} **c** 3.14^{03} **d** 9.03^{02}

Rounding

There are two main uses of rounding, both of which you have met before. One is to give an answer to a sensible degree of accuracy. The other is to enable you to make an estimate of the answer to a problem.

Example 7.3 Round each of the following numbers to **i** one decimal place and **ii** two decimal places.

a 7.356   **b** 13.978   **c** 0.2387

a 7.356 = 7.4 to one decimal place; 7.356 = 7.36 to two decimal places

b 13.978 = 14.0 to one decimal place; 13.978 = 13.98 to two decimal places

c 0.2387 = 0.2 to one decimal place; 0.2387 = 0.24 to two decimal places

Example 7.4 Round each of the following numbers to one significant figure.

a 18.67   **b** 3.761   **c** 7.95

a 18.67 = 20 to one significant figure

b 3.761 = 4 to one significant figure

c 7.95 = 8 to one significant figure

Example 7.5 Estimate the answer to each of the following.

a 11% of £598   **b** $\dfrac{23.7 + 69.3}{3.1 \times 3.2}$

The method is to round the numbers to one significant figure, which gives:

a 11% of £598 ≈ 10% of £600 = £60

b $\dfrac{23.7 + 69.3}{3.1 \times 3.2} \approx \dfrac{20 + 70}{3 \times 3} = \dfrac{90}{9} = 10$

Example 7.6 Which of each of the following is the most sensible answer?

a The distance from my house to the local post office: **i** 721.4 m,   **ii** 721 m or   **iii** 700 m.

b The time in which an athlete runs a 100 metre race: **i** 10.14 seconds, **ii** 10.1 seconds or **iii** 10 seconds.

a Distances are usually rounded to one or two significant figures. Hence, 700 m is the sensible answer.

b 100-metre times need to be accurate to the nearest hundredth of a second. Hence, 10.14 s is the sensible answer.

[**Note** An answer cannot be 'more accurate' than the accuracy of the numbers in the question.]

1 Round each of the following numbers to **i** one decimal place and **ii** two decimal places.

a 2.367	**b** 13.0813	**c** 8.907	**d** 20.029
e 0.999	**f** 4.0599	**g** 0.853	**h** 3.14159

2 Round each of the following numbers to one significant figure.

a 4560	**b** 941	**c** 3.09	**d** 42.6
e 0.999	**f** 5.598	**g** 31.7	**h** 298

3 Estimate the answer to each of the following. Where appropriate, round each answer to a sensible degree of accuracy.

a 9% of £278	**b** $23.2 \div 9.2$	**c** 12.3×0.53
d $\dfrac{23.1 + 57.3}{19.5 - 8.7}$	**e** $\dfrac{29.5 \times 3.2}{1.89 \times 3.14}$	**f** $\dfrac{45.0 \times 83.2}{21.7 - 9.8}$
g 12% of 450 kg	**h** $59.5 \div 3.1^2$	**i** $(3.95 \times 1.88)^2$
j 18% of 621 km	**k** 4.8% of £812	**l** 68×32

4 Round each of the following quantities to a sensible degree of accuracy.

a Average speed of a journey: 63.7 mph.

b Size of an angle in a right-angled triangle: 23.478°.

c Weight of a sack of potatoes: 46.89 kg.

d Time taken to boil an egg: 4 minutes 3.7 seconds.

e Time to run a marathon: 2 hours 32 minutes and 44 seconds.

f World record for running 100 metres: 9.78 seconds.

5 Use a calculator to work out each of the following. Then round each result to an appropriate degree of accuracy.

a $\dfrac{56.2 + 48.9}{17.8 - 12.5}$	**b** $\dfrac{12.7 \times 13.9}{8.9 \times 4.3}$	**c** $1 \div 32$
d 0.58^2	**e** $1 \div 45$	**f** $23.478 \div 0.123$

Extension Work

Below are four calculator displays rounded to one decimal place, four ordinary numbers and four standard form numbers which are rounded to three significant figures.

Match them up.

3.8^4	7.2^{-3}	3.8^{-4}	7.2^3

37 842	7234	0.000 3784	0.007 234
7.23×10^{-3}	3.78×10^4	3.78×10^{-4}	7.23×10^3

Recurring decimals

$$\frac{3}{8} = 0.375 \qquad \frac{2}{3} = 0.666\,666\dots \qquad \pi = 3.141\,59\dots$$

The decimals shown above are, from left to right, a **terminating decimal**, a **recurring decimal** and a **decimal** which never terminates or recurs. (This is called an **irrational number**, which you may meet in your GCSE course.)

Every recurring decimal can be written as a fraction.

To show a recurring decimal, a small dot is placed over the first and last of the recurring digits. For example:

$$\frac{5}{18} = 0.27\dot{7} \qquad \frac{4}{11} = 0.\dot{3}\dot{6} \qquad \frac{2}{7} = 0.\dot{2}85\,71\dot{4}$$

Example 7.7 ▷ Write each of the following fractions as a recurring decimal.

    a $\frac{5}{9}$ **b** $\frac{4}{7}$ **c** $\frac{7}{11}$

Use a calculator to divide each numerator by its denominator.

    a $\frac{5}{9} = 5 \div 9 = 0.555\,555\dots = 0.\dot{5}$

    b $\frac{4}{7} = 4 \div 7 = 0.571\,428\,5714\dots = 0.\dot{5}71\,42\dot{8}$

    c $\frac{7}{11} = 7 \div 11 = 0.636\,363\dots = 0.\dot{6}\dot{3}$

Example 7.8 ▷ Write each of these as a terminating decimal or a recurring decimal, as appropriate.

    a $\frac{3}{8}$ **b** $\frac{2}{3}$ **c** $\frac{3}{10}$ **d** $\frac{3}{11}$

    a $3 \div 8 = 0.375$. This is a terminating decimal.

    b $2 \div 3 = 0.666\,666\dots = 0.\dot{6}$. This is a recurring decimal.

    c $3 \div 10 = 0.3$. This is a terminating decimal.

    d $3 \div 11 = 0.272\,7272\dots = 0.\dot{2}\dot{7}$. This is a recurring decimal.

Exercise 7C

1   Write each of these as a terminating decimal or a recurring decimal, as appropriate.

    a $\frac{3}{20}$ **b** $\frac{1}{3}$ **c** $\frac{1}{6}$ **d** $\frac{5}{8}$ **e** $\frac{7}{10}$

    f $\frac{5}{12}$ **g** $\frac{2}{9}$ **h** $\frac{4}{15}$ **i** $\frac{1}{16}$ **j** $\frac{3}{5}$

2   Write each of the following fractions as a recurring decimal.

    a $\frac{2}{7}$ **b** $\frac{76}{101}$ **c** $\frac{23}{33}$ **d** $\frac{2}{3}$ **e** $\frac{5}{9}$

3   Write the ninths as recurring decimals: for example, $\frac{1}{9} = 0.\dot{1}$, $\frac{2}{9} = 0.\dot{2}$, … . Describe any patterns you see.

4   Write the elevenths as recurring decimals: for example, $\frac{1}{11} = 0.\dot{0}\dot{9}$, $\frac{2}{11} = 0.\dot{1}\dot{8}$, … .Describe any patterns you see.

5   Write the sevenths as recurring decimals: for example, $\frac{1}{7} = 0.\dot{1}42\,85\dot{7}$, $\frac{2}{7} = 0.\dot{2}85\,71\dot{4}$, … . Describe any patterns you see.

The thirteenths are recurring decimals. They always have six recurring digits which fit into one of two cycles. These are shown on the right.

For example: $\frac{1}{13} = 0.\dot{0}7692\dot{3}$ and $\frac{2}{13} = 0.\dot{1}5384\dot{6}$

Use the above diagrams to write the thirteenths as recurring decimals. The first two digits are given.

a $\frac{3}{13} = 0.23...$ **b** $\frac{4}{13} = 0.30...$ **c** $\frac{5}{13} = 0.38...$ **d** $\frac{6}{13} = 0.46...$

e $\frac{7}{13} = 0.53...$ **f** $\frac{8}{13} = 0.61...$ **g** $\frac{9}{13} = 0.69...$ **h** $\frac{10}{13} = 0.76...$

i $\frac{11}{13} = 0.84...$ **j** $\frac{12}{13} = 0.92...$

Multiplying decimals

This section will give you more practice in multiplying integers and decimals.

Example 7.9

Find each of the following.

a 0.3×0.05 **b** 900×0.4 **c** 50×0.04

a There are three decimal places in the multiplication, so there are three in the answer. Therefore, you have:
$$0.3 \times 0.05 = 0.015$$

b Rewrite as an equivalent product. That is:
$$900 \times 0.4 = 90 \times 4 = 360$$

c As in part **b**, giving: $50 \times 0.04 = 5 \times 0.4 = 2$

Example 7.10

Without using a calculator, work out 134×0.6.

There are several ways to do this. Three are shown (a column method and two box methods). Whichever method you use, you should first estimate the answer:
$$134 \times 0.6 \approx 100 \times 0.6 = 60$$

Remember also that there is one decimal place in the product, so there will be one in the answer.

In the first two methods, the decimal points are ignored in the multiplication and then placed in the answer.

Column method
```
   134
 ×   6
   804
   2 2
```

Box method 1

	100	30	4	Total
6	600	180	24	804

Box method 2

	100	30	4	Total
0.6	60	18	2.4	80.4

By all three methods the answer is 80.4.

Do not use a calculator to answer any of these questions.

1 Work out the answer to each of these.

a	0.3×0.6	**b**	0.5×0.5	**c**	0.9×0.7	**d**	0.6×0.6
e	0.9×0.8	**f**	0.7×0.6	**g**	0.5×0.8	**h**	0.4×0.4
i	0.7×0.7	**j**	0.9×0.3	**k**	0.4×0.8	**l**	0.3×0.2

2 Work out each of these. Show your working.

a	400×0.5	**b**	0.7×200	**c**	0.3×400	**d**	0.6×500
e	0.7×400	**f**	0.8×200	**g**	0.5×7000	**h**	0.3×4000
i	0.4×7000	**j**	300×0.09	**k**	900×0.01	**l**	900×0.04
m	600×0.1	**n**	700×0.01	**o**	800×0.001	**p**	900×0.0001

3 Work out each of these. Show your working.

a	0.002×500	**b**	0.03×0.04	**c**	0.02×800
d	400×600	**e**	40×0.006	**f**	0.08×4000

4 Work out the answer to each of the following. Use any method you are happy with. Show your working.

a	73×0.4	**b**	5.82×0.4	**c**	12.3×0.7	**d**	1.24×0.3
e	2.78×0.8	**f**	12.6×0.2	**g**	2.63×0.6	**h**	0.6×4.25

5 A rectangle is 2.46 m by 0.6 m. What is the area of the rectangle? Show your working.

Extension Work

1 Work out each of the following.

a 0.2^2 **b** 0.7^2 **c** $0.7^2 - 0.2^2$ **d** 0.5×0.9

2 Work out each of the following.

a 0.5^2 **b** 0.1^2 **c** $0.5^2 - 0.1^2$ **d** 0.6×0.4

3 Look for a connection between the calculations in parts **c** and **d** of Questions **1** and **2**. Then *write down* the answer to $0.8^2 - 0.2^2$. Check your answer with a calculator.

Dividing decimals

This section will give you more practice in dividing integers and decimals.

Example 7.11 ▶ Work out each of these.

  a $0.12 \div 0.3$ **b** $60 \div 0.15$

  a Simplify the division by rewriting it as equivalent divisions. In this case, keep multiplying both numbers by 10 until the divisor (0.3) becomes a simple whole number (3). This is equivalent to shifting the digits in both numbers to the left by the same amount. So, you have:

$$0.12 \div 0.3 = 1.2 \div 3$$
$$= 0.4$$

  b Rewriting as equivalent divisions gives:
$$60 \div 0.15 = 600 \div 1.5$$
$$= 6000 \div 15 = 400$$

Example 7.12 ▶ Work out each of these.

  a $32.8 \div 40$ **b** $7.2 \div 800$

  a Simplify the division by rewriting it as equivalent divisions. In this case, keep dividing both numbers by 10 until the divisor (40) becomes a simple whole number (4). This is equivalent to shifting the digits in both numbers to the right by the same amount. So, you have:

$$32.8 \div 40 = 3.28 \div 4$$

which can be worked out as a short division:

$$\begin{array}{r} 0.82 \\ \hline 4\overline{)3.28} \end{array}$$

  b Rewriting as equivalent divisions gives:
$$7.2 \div 800 = 0.72 \div 80$$
$$= 0.072 \div 8$$

which can be worked out as a short division:

$$\begin{array}{r} 0.009 \\ \hline 8\overline{)0.072} \end{array}$$

Example 7.13 ▶ Work out $4.32 \div 1.2$.

First, estimate the answer:
$$4.32 \div 1.2 \approx 4 \div 1 = 4$$

Write the problem as an equivalent problem without its decimal points ($432 \div 12$) and use repeated subtraction (chunking). This gives:

$$\begin{array}{rl} 432 & \\ -\,360 & (30 \times 12) \\ \hline 72 & \\ -\;\;72 & (6 \times 12) \\ \hline 0 & (36 \times 12) \end{array}$$

Insert the decimal point in the quotient (36), which gives $4.32 \div 1.2 = 3.6$.

Do not use a calculator to answer any of these questions.

1 Work out each of the following. Show your working.

   a $0.36 \div 0.2$ **b** $0.48 \div 0.5$ **c** $0.45 \div 0.2$ **d** $0.18 \div 0.3$

   e $0.24 \div 0.2$ **f** $0.48 \div 0.3$ **g** $0.39 \div 0.3$ **h** $0.24 \div 0.5$

2 Work out each of the following. Show your working.

   a $600 \div 0.4$ **b** $500 \div 0.2$ **c** $400 \div 0.8$ **d** $300 \div 0.2$

   e $60 \div 0.15$ **f** $50 \div 0.25$ **g** $500 \div 0.2$ **h** $40 \div 0.4$

3 Work out each of the following. Show your working.

   a $3.2 \div 4$ **b** $2.8 \div 40$ **c** $24 \div 40$ **d** $36 \div 90$

   e $4.8 \div 80$ **f** $4.8 \div 20$ **g** $3.5 \div 70$ **h** $0.16 \div 40$

4 Work out each of the following. Use any method you are happy with.

   a $3.36 \div 1.4$ **b** $1.56 \div 2.4$ **c** $5.4 \div 3.6$ **d** $20.8 \div 5.2$

   e $22.1 \div 6.5$ **f** $2.72 \div 3.4$ **g** $4.6 \div 23$ **h** $2.16 \div 0.24$

5 A rectangle has an area of 3.78 cm². The length is 2.7 cm. Calculate the width.

Extension Work

1 Given that $46 \times 34 = 1564$, work out each of these.

   a 46×17 **b** 4.6×34 **c** $1564 \div 0.34$ **d** $15.64 \div 4.6$

2 Given that $39 \times 32 = 1248$, work out each of these.

   a 3.9×32 **b** 13×32 **c** 3900×0.32 **d** 0.0039×32

3 Given that $2.8 \times 0.55 = 1.540$, work out each of these.

   a 28×55 **b** $154 \div 55$ **c** $15.4 \div 0.28$ **d** 0.028×5500

Efficient calculations

It is important that you know how to use your calculator. You should be able to use the basic functions (×, ÷, +, −) and the square, square root and brackets keys. You have also met the memory and sign-change keys. This exercise introduces the fraction and power keys.

Example 7.14   Use a calculator to work out:

    a $(1\frac{1}{2} - \frac{3}{4}) \times \frac{2}{3}$ **b** $\dfrac{\frac{1}{5} + 1\frac{3}{4}}{1\frac{1}{2} - \frac{3}{10}}$

    a Using the fraction button $a\frac{b}{c}$, key in the calculation as:

$$(\quad 1 \quad a\tfrac{b}{c} \quad 1 \quad a\tfrac{b}{c} \quad 2 \quad - \quad 3 \quad a\tfrac{b}{c} \quad 4 \quad) \quad \times \quad 2 \quad a\tfrac{b}{c} \quad 3 \quad =$$

        The display should show $1 \lrcorner 2$, which represents the fraction $\frac{1}{2}$. Note that the way this is keyed in may be different on your calculator.

    b Using brackets and the fraction buttons gives an answer of $1\frac{5}{8}$.

        (Shown in some displays as $1 \lrcorner 5 \lrcorner 8$.)

Example 7.15   Use a calculator to work out:

    a 3^7 **b** $\sqrt[3]{125}$ **c** $\sqrt{6.5^2 - 2.5^2}$

    a Using the power key, which may look like x^y, the answer should be 2187.

    b This can be keyed in as $\boxed{1}\ \boxed{2}\ \boxed{5}\ \boxed{\sqrt[3]{\ }}\ \boxed{=}$ or $\boxed{\sqrt[3]{\ }}\ \boxed{1}\ \boxed{2}\ \boxed{5}\ \boxed{=}$

        or $\boxed{1}\ \boxed{2}\ \boxed{5}\ \boxed{x^y}\ \boxed{(}\ \boxed{1}\ \boxed{a\tfrac{b}{c}}\ \boxed{3}\ \boxed{)}\ \boxed{=}$

        The answer is 5. Make sure you can use your calculator to find this answer.

    c Using the square root, bracket and square keys, the answer should be 6. For example, the following are two ways to key the problem into the calculator:

$$\sqrt{\ }\ (\ 6\ .\ 5\ x^2\ -\ 2\ .\ 5\ x^2\ )\ =$$

        or $(\ 6\ .\ 5\ x^2\ -\ 2\ .\ 5\ x^2\ )\ \sqrt{\ }\ =$

Exercise 7F

Use your calculator to work out each of these questions.

1 **a** $\dfrac{22.7 - 7.1}{2.72 + 2.48}$ **b** $\sqrt{6.1^2 - 1.1^2}$ **c** $5.75 \div (4.6 - 2.1)$

2 Give each answer as a mixed number or a fraction in its simplest form, as appropriate.

    a $\frac{1}{8} + \frac{1}{3} + \frac{5}{6}$ **b** $2\frac{2}{5} + 2\frac{3}{10}$ **c** $\frac{2}{3} \times \frac{9}{14}$

    d $(2\frac{1}{2} + 2\frac{3}{4}) \times \frac{4}{5}$ **e** $\dfrac{1\frac{1}{5} - \frac{3}{4}}{\frac{1}{2} + \frac{1}{10}}$ **f** $\dfrac{2\frac{1}{3} - 1\frac{1}{4}}{1\frac{3}{8} - \frac{5}{6}}$

    g $(\frac{3}{8})^2$ **h** $\sqrt{3\frac{1}{9} - 1\frac{1}{3}}$ **i** $(1\frac{1}{4} + \frac{7}{8}) \div \frac{5}{8}$

3 Where necessary, round the answers to two decimal places.

    a 3^5 **b** 3.2^2 **c** $\sqrt[3]{2197}$

    d $\sqrt{2^5 + 5^2}$ **e** 4^5 **f** $3 \times (2.12)^3$

    g 4×1.8^2 **h** $(4 \times 1.8)^2$ **i** $\sqrt{5.3^2 - 2.3^2}$

4 **a** Add 3 hours and 15 minutes to 2 hours and 50 minutes.

b Subtract 1 hour and 55 minutes from 3 hours and 25 minutes.

c Multiply 1 hour and 20 minutes by 4.

Extension Work

Choose a number between 1 and 2, say 1.5. Key it into the calculator display.

Perform the following sequence of key presses:

Note The **1/x** key may be in the form x^{-1}. This is called the **reciprocal** key.

After the sequence has been performed, the display should show 0.4.

Repeat the above sequence of key presses. The display should now show 0.714 … .

Keep repeating the above sequence of key presses until the first three decimal places of the number in the display starts to repeat.

Solving problems

Example 7.16 Which jar of jam offers the better value?

The smaller jar gives 454 ÷ 89 = 5.1 grams/penny.

The larger jar gives 2000 ÷ 400 = 5 grams/penny.

So, the smaller jar offers the better value.

Example 7.17 A bag of identical marbles weighs 375 grams. Seven marbles are taken out. The bag then weighs 270 grams. How many marbles were in the bag to start with?

The difference in weights is 375 – 270 = 105 g. This is the weight of seven marbles, so one marble weighs

105 ÷ 7 = 15 g

Hence, the number of marbles originally in the bag is given by:

375 ÷ 15 = 25

1 Two families went to the cinema. It cost the Ahmed family of one adult and two children £11.50. It cost the Smith family of two adults and two children £16. What is the cost of an adult's ticket and a child's ticket?

2 What fraction is halfway between $\frac{3}{5}$ and $\frac{9}{10}$?

3 This is the charge for hiring a car.

   a   How much will it cost to hire the car for 5 days?

   b   John pays £133.50 for car hire. For how many days did he hire the car?

CAR HIRE
£25 plus
£15.50 per day

4 Leisureways sell Kayenno trainers for £69.99 but give 10% discount for Running Club members. All Sports sell the same trainers for £75 but are having a sale for which everything is reduced by 15%. In which shop are the trainers cheaper?

5 A supermarket sells crisps in different sized packets. An ordinary bag contains 30 g and costs 28p. A large bag contains 100 g and costs 90p. A jumbo bag contains 250 g and costs £2.30. Which bag is the best value? You must show all your working.

6 A cash-and-carry sells crisps in boxes. A 12-packet box costs £3.00. An 18-packet box costs £5.00. A 30-packet box costs £8.00. Which box gives the best value?

7 A box of chocolate has three soft-centred chocolates for every two hard-centred chocolates. There are 40 chocolates altogether in the box. How many of them are soft-centred?

8 Davy is twice as old as Arnie. The sum of their ages is 36 years. How old are they?

9 Fibonacci sequences are formed by adding the previous two numbers to get the next number. For example:

   1, 1, 2, 3, 5, 8, 13, 21, 34, 55, ...

   a   Write down the next three terms of the Fibonacci sequence that starts 2, 2, 4, 6, 10, 16, ...

   b   Work out the missing values of this sequence: 2, 4, 6, ..., 16, ..., ..., 68... .

   c   Work out the first three terms of this sequence: ..., ..., ..., 0, 1, 1, 2, 3, 5, 8, ...

10 A recipe for marmalade uses 65 grams of oranges for every 100 grams of marmalade. Mary has 10 kilograms of fruit. How many 454-gram jars of marmalade can Mary make?

Choose a two-digit number such as 18.

Multiply the units digit by 3 and add the tens digit, which give:

$3 \times 8 + 1 = 25$

Repeat with the new number:

$3 \times 5 + 2 = 17$

Keep repeating the procedure until the numbers start repeating, namely:

$17 \to 22 \to 8 \to 24 \to \dots$

Show the chains on a poster. For example:

What you need to know for level 4

- How to add and subtract decimals with up to two decimal places
- How to round numbers to the nearest 10, 100 and 1000

What you need to know for level 5

- How to multiply and divide integers and decimal numbers
- How to estimate the results of calculations
- How to use the bracket, square, square root and sign-change keys on your calculator
- How to round numbers to one decimal place

National Curriculum SATs questions

LEVEL 4

1 *1999 Paper 2*

Here are some number cards. | 1 | | 7 | | 3 | | 5 |

Use some of the four cards to make numbers that are as close as possible to the numbers shown.

For example: 80 → | 7 | | 5 |, 30 → | 3 | | 1 |

50 →   60 →   4000 →   1500 →   1600 →

2   *1998 Paper 2*

The table shows the lengths of some rivers to the nearest km.

River	Severn	Thames	Trent	Wye	Dee
Length	354	346	297	215	113

a   Write the length of each river rounded to the nearest 100 km. Which two rivers have the same length to the nearest 100 km?

b   Write the length of each river rounded to the nearest 10 km. Which two rivers have the same length to the nearest 10 km?

c   There is a river that is not on the list. It has a length of 200 km to the nearest 100 km and a length of 150 km to the nearest 10 km. Give one possible length of the river to the nearest km.

d   Two more rivers have different lengths to the nearest km. They both have a length of 250 km to the nearest 10 km, but their lengths to the nearest 100 km are different. Give a possible length of each river to the nearest km.

LEVEL 5

3   *2002 Paper 1*

a   Peter's height is 0.9 m. Lucy is 0.3 m taller than Peter. What is Lucy's height?

b   Lee's height is 1.45 m. Misha is 0.3 m shorter than Lee. What is Misha's height?

c   Zita's height is 1.7 m. What is Zita's height in centimetres?

4   *2002 Paper 2*

Some people use yards to measure length.

The diagram shows one way to change yards to metres.

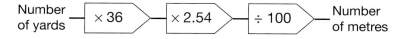

Number of yards — $\times 36$ — $\times 2.54$ — $\div 100$ — Number of metres

a   Change 100 yards to metres.

b   Change 100 metres to yards.

Show your working.

CHAPTER 8 Algebra 4

This chapter is going to show you

- how to find the highest common factor (HCF)
- how to find the lowest common multiple (LCM)
- how to find prime factors
- the significance of m and c in equations of the form $y = mx + c$

What you should already know

- What factors and multiples are
- First ten prime numbers
- How to plot points and draw a straight-line graph

LCM and HCF

Look at these diagrams.

15 18 21

4 8 12 16 20 24 28 32

9

3 6 9 27 30

18   42

9   1   14

2   3   7   21

18   6   42

This shows the common multiples of 3 and 4.

Which is the **lowest common multiple (LCM)**?

This shows the common factors of 18 and 42.

Which is the **highest common factor (HCM)**?

What is a multiple?

Multiples are best shown with examples.
Look at Examples 8.1 and 8.2

Example 8.1 ▷ List the first ten multiples of 5.

Any whole number multiplied by 5 is a multiple of 5.

So, the first ten are:

5 10 15 20 25 30 35 40 45 50

Example 8.2 ▷ Is 105 a multiple of 3?

If 105 can be divided by 3 exactly, it must be a multiple of 3.

Now, 105 ÷ 3 = 35. Hence, 105 is a multiple of 3.

Lowest common multiple (LCM)

Any pair of numbers has many common multiples. The lowest of these is called the LCM. This can be found by listing the first few multiples of both numbers until you see the first common number.

Example 8.3 ▷ Find the LCM of 6 and 8.

Write out the first few multiples of each number:

　　6　12　18　**24**　30　36　42　**48**　54 …
　　8　16　**24**　32　40　**48**　56 …

You can see which are the common multiples, the lowest of which is 24.

So, **24** is the LCM of 6 and 8.

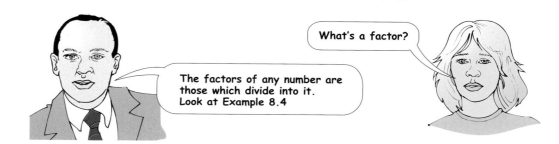

What's a factor?

The factors of any number are those which divide into it. Look at Example 8.4

Example 8.4 ▷ Write down the factors of 24.

The factors are best found in pairs, for example:
　　1 × 24　2 × 12　3 × 8　4 × 6

Putting these into numerical order gives:
　　1　2　3　4　6　8　12　24

Highest common factor (HCF)

The highest common factor of two numbers is found by following these three steps.
- List the factors of each number.
- Look for and list the common factors.
- Look for the highest common factor in this list.

Example 8.5 ▷ Find the HCF of 18 and 42.

List the factors of each number:
　　1　**2**　**3**　**6**　9　18
　　1　**2**　**3**　**6**　7　14　21　42

You can see that the HCF of 18 and 42 is **6**.

1 Write down the numbers in the list below which are multiples of:

    a   2   **b**   3   **c**   5   **d**   9

         12   6   21   20   63   88   9   55   27   4   65

2 Write down the first ten multiples of:

    a   3   **b**   5   **c**   7   **d**   10   **e**   12

3 Use your answers to Question **2** to help you to find the LCM of:

    a   3 and 5   **b**   5 and 10   **c**   7 and 10   **d**   10 and 12

4 Write down all the factors of:

    a   4   **b**   21   **c**   27   **d**   30   **e**   36

5 Use your answers to Question **4** to help you to find the HCF of:

    a   12 and 21   **b**   12 and 36   **c**   25 and 30   **d**   27 and 36

6 Find the LCM of:

    a   3 and 7   **b**   6 and 12   **c**   4 and 7   **d**   8 and 12

    e   9 and 15   **f**   8 and 20   **g**   9 and 30   **h**   10 and 15

7 Find the HCF of:

    a   16 and 20   **b**   8 and 30   **c**   10 and 15   **d**   20 and 24

    e   3 and 12   **f**   6 and 16   **g**   27 and 36   **h**   30 and 45

8   **a**   What is the HCF and LCM of:

         i   3, 5   **ii**   4, 7   **iii**   3, 8

    b   Two numbers, x and y, have an HCF of 1. What is the LCM of x and y?

    a   What is the HCF and LCM of:

         i   4 , 8   **ii**   5 , 10   **iii**   3 , 12

    b   Two numbers, x and y, where y is bigger than x, have an HCF of x.
         What is the LCM of x and y?

    c   Two numbers, x and y, have an HCF of $\frac{xy}{2}$. What is special about the two numbers?

Powers and roots

Square numbers

The area of a square whose sides have a length of x is $x \times x$, which is written as x^2. This is why x^2 is called 'x squared' or the 'square of x'. Hence, when any number is multiplied by itself, the answer is called the **square of the number** or the **number squared**.

     x

     Area x^2 x

As with x^2, the short way to write the square of any number is, for example:

6 squared $= (6 \times 6) = 6^2$

13 squared $= (13 \times 13) = 13^2$

Square roots

Taking the **square root** is the inverse (opposite) of squaring. Hence, the square root of any given number is a number which, when multiplied by itself, produces the given number.

A square root is shown by the sign $\sqrt{\ }$. For example, $\sqrt{9} = 3$.

Example 8.6

Since $5^2 = 25$, then $\sqrt{25} = 5$

$9^2 = 81$, then $\sqrt{81} = 9$

$11^2 = 121$, then $\sqrt{121} = 11$

Cubed numbers

The volume of a cube whose sides have a length of x is $x \times x \times x$, which is written as x^3. This is why x^3 is called 'x cubed' or the cube of x. Hence, when any number is multiplied by itself, and again by itself, the answer is called the **cube of the number** or the **number cubed**.

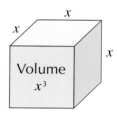

Cube roots

Taking the **cube root** is the inverse (opposite) of cubing. Hence the cube root of any given number is a number which, when multiplied by itself twice, produces the given number.

A cube root is shown by the sign $\sqrt[3]{\ }$. For example, $\sqrt[3]{27} = 3$.

Example 8.7

Since $2^3 = 8$, then $\sqrt[3]{8} = 2$

$5^3 = 125$, then $\sqrt[3]{125} = 5$

Example 8.8

Work out each of these: **a** 7^2 **b** 5^3

a $7^2 = 7 \times 7 = 49$

b $5^3 = 5 \times 5 \times 5 = 125$

Example 8.9

Work out each of these: **a** $\sqrt{100}$ **b** $\sqrt[3]{64}$

a Think of the number which, multiplied by itself, makes 100. It is 10.
Hence $\sqrt{100} = 10$.

b Using trial and improvement gives the following:

$1 \times 1 \times 1 = 1$ $2 \times 2 \times 2 = 8$ $3 \times 3 \times 3 = 27$ $4 \times 4 \times 4 = 64$

Hence, $\sqrt[3]{64} = 4$.

1 The diagrams on pages 118 and 119 show a square and a cube, both with a side length of x. Copy and complete this table.

Side length, x	1 cm	2 cm	3 cm	4 cm	5 cm	6 cm	7 cm	8 cm	9 cm	10 cm
Area of square	1 cm²									
Volume of cube	1 cm³									

2 Use the table in Question **1** to work out each of the following:

    a $\sqrt{1}$ **b** $\sqrt{4}$ **c** $\sqrt{9}$ **d** $\sqrt{36}$ **e** $\sqrt{49}$

    f $\sqrt[3]{1}$ **g** $\sqrt[3]{27}$ **h** $\sqrt[3]{216}$ **i** $\sqrt[3]{8}$ **j** $\sqrt[3]{343}$

3 Find the positive value of x that makes each of the following equations true.

    a $x^2 = 25$ **b** $x^2 = 49$ **c** $x^2 = 81$ **d** $x^2 = 1$

    e $x^2 = 121$ **f** $x^2 = 64$ **g** $x^2 = 100$ **h** $x^2 = 1\,000\,000$

4 Find the value of each of the following.

    a $11^2 + 11^3$ **b** $12^2 + 12^3$ **c** $13^2 + 13^3$

5 For each number in the circle, match it with its square root in the rectangle. Pair them up and write down as for example, $\sqrt{100} = 10$.

    19   18   13   14   400 196

    15   21   20   17   324 256

      22   16   12   225 361

                            289

6 **a** Explain how you can tell that $\sqrt{12}$ is between 3 and 4.

    b Explain how you can tell that $\sqrt{40}$ is between 6 and 7.

    c What two consecutive whole numbers is $\sqrt{60}$ between?

    d What two consecutive whole numbers is $\sqrt{90}$ between?

7 **a** Explain how you can tell that $\sqrt[3]{5}$ is between 1 and 2.

    b Explain how you can tell that $\sqrt[3]{19}$ is between 2 and 3.

    c What two consecutive whole numbers is $\sqrt[3]{100}$ between?

    d What two consecutive whole numbers is $\sqrt[3]{50}$ between?

How many squares are there on a chessboard?

The answer is not 64!

For example in this square [figure] there are five squares,

four this size □ and one this size □.

In this square [figure] there are 14 squares,

nine this size □ four this size □ and one this size □.

By drawing increasingly larger 'chessboards', work out how many squares there are and see if you can spot the pattern.

A computer spreadsheet is useful for this activity.

Prime factors

A prime number can only be divided exactly by itself and one. The first ten prime numbers are: 2, 3, 5, 7, 11, 13, 17, 19, 23, 29. You need to know these.

The prime factors of a number are the prime numbers which, when multiplied together, give that number.

There are two ways to find prime factors.

Example 8.10

Find the prime factors of 12.

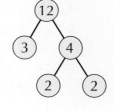

Using a prime factor tree, split 12 into 3×4.

Since 4 can be split into 2×2, this gives:

$12 = 3 \times 2 \times 2$

Use powers to simplify the answer:

$12 = 3 \times 2^2$

Example 8.11

Find the prime factors of 40.

Use the divide method. That is, dividing by the smallest prime number:

$$\begin{array}{c|c} 2 & 40 \\ 2 & 20 \\ 2 & 10 \\ 5 & 5 \\ \hline & 1 \end{array}$$

So, $40 = 2 \times 2 \times 2 \times 5$ which gives $2^3 \times 5$ (again using powers to simplify the answer).

What use are prime factors?

One of the main uses is to help to find the HCF and LCM pairs of numbers

Example 8.12

Use prime factors to find the HCF and the LCM of 36 and 42.

Breaking down the two numbers into prime factors gives:

$36 = 2 \times 2 \times 3 \times 3$ and $42 = 2 \times 3 \times 7$

2×3 is common to both sets of prime factors as shown in the central part of the diagram. But the remaining prime factors, 2×3 and 7, belong respectively to each of the original numbers, as shown in the outer parts of the diagram.

Therefore, the HCF is the product $2 \times 3 = 6$.

And the LCM is the product of all the prime factors:

$2 \times 2 \times 3 \times 3 \times 7 = 252$

36   **42**

2   2   7
3   3

Exercise 8C

1 These are the prime factors of different numbers. What are the numbers?

 a $2 \times 2 \times 5$ **b** $2 \times 3 \times 3$ **c** $3 \times 3 \times 5$ **d** $2 \times 3 \times 5$

 e $2 \times 2 \times 2 \times 5$ **f** $2 \times 3 \times 3 \times 5$ **g** $2 \times 2 \times 5 \times 5$ **h** $2 \times 3 \times 5 \times 5$

2 What numbers are represented by each of the following sets of prime factors?

 a $2^3 \times 7$ **b** $2^2 \times 3^2$ **c** $2 \times 3^2 \times 5$ **d** 3×5^2

3 Use a prime factor tree to find the prime factors of each of the following numbers.

 a 15   **b** 20   **c** 24   **d** 32   **e** 35

 f 18   **g** 21   **h** 28   **i** 36   **j** 45

4 Use the division method to find the prime factors of each of the following numbers.

 a 160   **b** 144   **c** 90   **d** 150   **e** 196

 f 180   **g** 216   **h** 108   **i** 126   **j** 450

5 Using the diagrams below work out the HCF and the LCM of each pair of numbers.

 a   **40**   **60**   **b**   **36**   **48**   **c**   **45**   **60**

 2   2   3   3   2   2   3   3   2
      2   2   2   3
      5   3   5   2

6 The prime factors of 180 are $2 \times 2 \times 3 \times 3 \times 5$. The prime factors of 675 are $3 \times 3 \times 3 \times 5 \times 5$.

    a Put these numbers into a diagram like those shown in Question **5**.

    b Use the diagram to work out the HCF and the LCM of 180 and 675.

7 The prime factors of 112 are $2 \times 2 \times 2 \times 2 \times 7$. The prime factors of 420 are $2 \times 2 \times 3 \times 5 \times 7$.

    a Put these numbers into a diagram like those shown in Question **5**.

    b Use the diagram to work out the HCF and the LCM of 112 and 420.

8 Use their prime factors to work out the HCF and the LCM of each pair of numbers.

    a 150 and 125   **b** 240 and 420   **c** 90 and 135

Extension Work

  a How many prime numbers less than 100 are one more than a multiple of 6 (for example, 13)?

  b How many prime numbers less than 100 are one less than a multiple of 6 (for example, 11)?

  c How many prime numbers less than 100 are neither one less nor one more than a multiple of 6?

  d What do the answers to parts **a**, **b** and **c** suggest about prime numbers greater than 3?

Graphs of equations of the form $y = mx + c$

You have met already graphs plotted from functions with the form $y = mx + c$, where m and c are any numbers (see pages 48–50). These are always straight-line graphs.

Example 8.13

Draw a graph of the equation $y = 3x + 1$.

First, construct a table of easy values for x as shown below.

x	0	1	2	3
$y = 3x + 1$	1	4	7	10

Next, draw the axes on graph paper. Mark the values for x on the horizontal axis, and those for y on the vertical axis.

Then plot the points given in the table, and join them with a straight line.

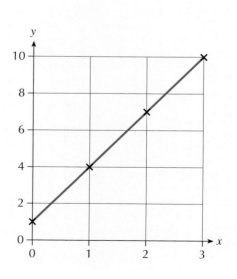

Each question in this exercise is a short investigation into the positions of the graphs of equations written in the form $y = mx + c$. After completing the investigations, you should find something very important and useful about the values of m and c, which will help you to see where the straight-line graph lies for each equation.

1 a Copy and complete the table below for the equations shown.

x	0	1	2	3
$y = x + 1$	1			
$y = x + 2$		3		
$y = x + 3$			5	
$y = x + 4$				7

b Draw a grid with its x-axis from 0 to 3 and its y-axis from 0 to 7.

c Draw the graph for each equation in the table above.

d What do you notice about each graph?

e Use what you have noticed to draw the graphs of these equations:

  i $y = x + 5$ **ii** $y = x + 0.5$

2 a Copy and complete the table below for the equations shown.

x	0	1	2	3
$y = 2x + 1$	1			
$y = 2x + 2$		4		
$y = 2x + 3$			7	
$y = 2x + 4$				10

b Draw a grid with its x-axis from 0 to 3 and its y-axis from 0 to 10.

c Draw the graph for each equation in the table above.

d What do you notice about each graph?

e If you draw a graph of $y = mx + c$, where m and c are any numbers, what does the value of c tell you about the straight-line graph?

f Use what you have noticed to draw the graphs of these equations:

  i $y = 2x + 5$ **ii** $y = 2x + 0.5$

3 a Copy and complete the table below for the equations shown.

x	0	1	2	3
$y = x$	0			
$y = 2x$		2		
$y = 3x$			6	
$y = 4x$				12

b Draw a grid with its x-axis from 0 to 3 and its y-axis from 0 to 12.

c Draw the graph for each equation in the table above.

d What do you notice about each graph?

e Use what you have noticed to draw the graphs of these equations:

    i $y = 5x$ **ii** $y = 0.5x$

4 **a** Copy and complete the table below for the equations shown.

x	0	1	2	3
$y = x + 4$	4			
$y = 2x + 4$		6		
$y = 3x + 4$			10	
$y = 4x + 4$				16

b Draw a grid with its x-axis from 0 to 3 and its y-axis from 0 to 16.

c Draw the graph for each equation in the table above.

d What do you notice about each graph?

e If you draw a graph of $y = mx + c$, where m and c are any numbers, what does the value of m tell you about the straight-line graph?

f Use what you have noticed to draw the graphs of these equations:

    i $y = 5x + 4$ **ii** $y = 0.5x + 4$

Extension Work

1 Draw the graphs of each of the following equations by finding suitable coordinates and plotting them.

    a $y = 5 - x$ **b** $y = 10 - x$ **c** $y = 12 - x$

2 What do your answers to Question 1 suggest about the graphs from equations of the form $y = A - x$?

What you need to know for level 4

- How to find the square of a number and a simple square root
- Be able to plot a few points on a grid and draw a graph

What you need to know for level 5

- How to find common factors
- How to find common multiples
- How to find the prime factors of numbers less than 100
- Be able to draw a graph from any simple linear equation

National Curriculum SATs questions

LEVEL 4

1 *2002 Paper 1*

There are four different ways to put
6 students into equal-size groups.

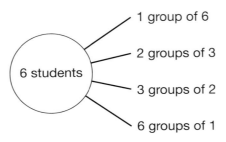

1 group of 6

2 groups of 3

3 groups of 2

6 groups of 1

6 students

a Copy the diagram on the right. Then show
the five different ways to put 16 students
into equal-size groups.

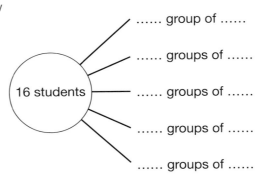

16 students

...... group of ......

...... groups of ......

...... groups of ......

...... groups of ......

...... groups of ......

b Copy the numbers below and then circle those which are factors of twelve.

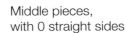

1	2	3	4	5	6
7	8	9	20	11	12

LEVEL 5

2 *1998 Paper 1*

A jigsaw has three different sorts of piece.

Corner pieces,
with 2 straight sides

Edge pieces,
with 1 straight side

Middle pieces,
with 0 straight sides

a This jigsaw has 24 pieces altogether, in 4 rows of 6. Copy and complete the table below to
show how many of each sort of piece this jigsaw has.

Corner pieces:	......
Edge pieces:	......
Middle pieces:	......
Total:	24

b Another jigsaw has 42 pieces altogether, in 6 rows of 7. Copy and complete the table below to show how many of each sort of piece this jigsaw has.

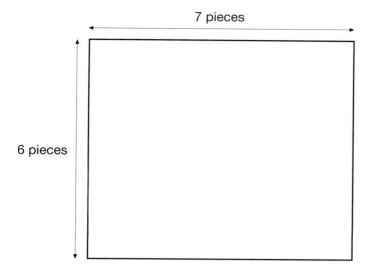

7 pieces

6 pieces

Corner pieces:	......
Edge pieces:	......
Middle pieces:	......
Total:	42

c A square jigsaw has 64 middle pieces.

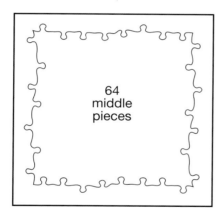

64 middle pieces

Corner pieces:	......
Edge pieces:	......
Middle pieces:	64
Total:	......

Copy and complete the table above to show how many of each sort of piece the square jigsaw has, and the total number of pieces.

Remember that the total must be a square number.

This chapter is going to show you

- how to record mutually exclusive outcomes
- how to solve probability problems involving mutually exclusive outcomes
- how to use a two-way table or sample space diagram to calculate probabilities
- how to work out probabilities in different situations
- how to obtain estimates of probability

What you should already know

- Some basic ideas about chance and probability
- How to use a probability scale
- How to calculate probabilities for single events

Mutually exclusive events

Toss a coin twice and then make a list of all possible outcomes (also called events).

First throw	Second throw
Head	Head
Head	Tail
Tail	Head
Tail	Tail

There are four different outcomes. They are called **mutually exclusive events**, because they cannot happen at the same time.

For example, when you roll a dice, the outcome cannot be both an even number and an odd number at the same time. So, the events 'even' and 'odd' are mutually exclusive.

When you roll a dice once, the outcome could be both 'odd' and 'greater than 3', because you could get 5. So, the events 'odd' and 'greater than 3' are **not mutually exclusive** because they overlap and can both happen at the same time.

Example 9.1

Example 9.1 ⊳

continued

Here is a list of events about the shopper.

> Event A: He chooses bread.
> Event B: He chooses something which needs cooking.
> Event C: He chooses white bread.
> Event D: He chooses meat.

The shopper chooses only one of these four items. List the outcomes of each event. Then state which of these pairs of events are mutually exclusive.

a A and B   **b** A and C   **c** D and A   **d** B and D

A	B	C	D
White bread	Sausages	White bread	Sausages
Brown bread	Bacon		Bacon
	Eggs		

a A and B are different, so these events are mutually exclusive.

b A and C have a common outcome, white bread. So, these events are not mutually exclusive.

c D and A are different, so these events are mutually exclusive.

d B and D have a common outcome, meat. So, these events are not mutually exclusive.

Exercise 9A

1 Look back at the Example 9.1.

   a On a particular day, the shopper buys *two* different items. List all the possible combinations he could choose.

   b On a particular day, the shopper buys *three* different items. List all the possible combinations he could choose.

2 A number square contains the numbers from 1 to 100.

1	2	3	4	5	6	7	8	9	10
11	12	13	14	15	16	17	18	19	20
21	22	23	24	25	26	27	28	29	30
31	32	33	34	35	36	37	38	39	40
41	42	43	44	45	46	47	48	49	50
51	52	53	54	55	56	57	58	59	60
61	62	63	64	65	66	67	68	69	70
71	72	73	74	75	76	77	78	79	80
81	82	83	84	85	86	87	88	89	90
91	92	93	94	95	96	97	98	99	100

Numbers are chosen from the number square. Here is a list of events.

> Event A: A number chosen is less than 20.
>
> Event B: A number chosen is greater than 80.
>
> Event C: An even number is chosen.
>
> Event D: An odd number is chosen.
>
> Event E: A number with only one digit is chosen.
>
> Event F: A number is chosen which is a multiple of 10 (10, 20, 30, 40, …).
>
> Event G: A number is chosen which is a square number (1, 4, 9, 16, …).

State whether each of the following pairs of events are mutually exclusive or not.

a	A and B	**b**	A and C	**c**	B and C	**d**	C and D
e	B and F	**f**	C and F	**g**	C and G	**h**	D and E
i	D and G	**j**	E and F	**k**	E and G	**l**	F and G

3 In a raffle a person can buy red, yellow or blue tickets. She decides to buy two tickets. List all the possible combinations that she could choose. State which are mutually exclusive.

4 There are red, yellow and blue counters in a bag.

Event A: Choosing a red counter.

Event B: Choosing a yellow counter.

Event C: Choosing a counter that is not blue.

State which of these events are mutually exclusive and which events are not mutually exclusive, giving a reason for each answer.

a A and B   **b** A and C   **c** B and C

5 Each of these spinners is spun once and the scores are multiplied together.

a Complete the table to show the different pairs of scores.

Spinner 1	Spinner 2	Total score
1	2	2
1	4	4
1	6	6

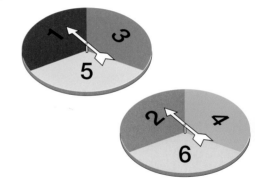

b Complete this statement.

Odd × Even = ...

Extension Work

Imagine a Formula 1 race between two racing cars (called A and B). They could finish the race in two different ways, AB or BA.

Now look at a three-car race. How many ways can they finish the race?

Extend this problem to four cars, and so on. Put your results into a table. See if you can work out a pattern to predict how many different ways a ten-car race could finish.

When you have finished this, you can explore what the factorial (!) button does on a calculator. (This may help you to solve the racing car problem.)

Calculating probabilities

Look at the spinners. Which one is most likely to land on red? Remember, the answer is not how many times a colour appears, but the probability that it will appear.

$$\text{Probability of event} = \frac{\text{Number of successes}}{\text{Total number of outcomes}}$$

Sometimes you have to look at more than one event. To do this you can use diagrams, called **sample spaces**, to record the possible outcomes. Look at the sample space for two coins.

	Head	Tail
Head	H,H	H,T
Tail	T,H	T,T

You can now work out the probability of throwing two Heads.

The diagram shows that there is only one way of getting two Heads. It also shows that there are four possible outcomes altogether.

So, the probability is $\frac{1}{4}$.

Example 9.2 ▷

A coin is tossed and a dice is rolled.

a Use a sample space diagram to show all the possible outcomes.

b What is the probability of tossing a Head and rolling a 6?

a

	1	2	3	4	5	6
Head	H, 1	H, 2	H, 3	H, 4	H, 5	H, 6
Tail	T, 1	T, 2	T, 3	T, 4	T, 5	T, 6

b Head and 6 is one of the 12 spaces on the diagram, so the probability is $\frac{1}{12}$.

Example 9.3 ▷

An ice-cream man sells vanilla, chocolate and strawberry flavours. A girl buys an ice-cream, saying to the man: 'You can choose the flavours.'

a What is the probability that the girl gets her favourite flavour if she buys a single scoop?

b She asks for two scoops, each scoop a different flavour. Make a list of the different combinations she could buy.

a She has only one favourite flavour, so the probability that she gets that one out of three flavours = $\frac{1}{3}$.

b Vanilla and chocolate

Vanilla and strawberry

Chocolate and strawberry

You could also list them in reverse order, as well. This would imply that the scoops are the opposite way round.

Exercise 9B

1 A set of cards are numbered 1 to 20. One card is picked at random. Give the probability for each of the following cases.

    a Even

    b Has only one digit

    c Has 1 on it

    d Has 2 on it

    e Is less than 5

    f Is greater than 8

    g Is a multiple of 3 (3, 6, 9, …)

2 These two spinners are spun. The scores on the spinners are added together to get the total score.

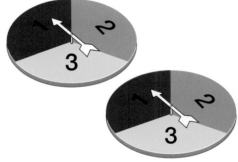

    a Copy and complete the sample space diagram for the total scores.

	1	2	3
1	2		
2			
3			

    b Write down the probability of a total score of 4.

    c Write down the probability of a total greater than 30.

3 A bag contains two red, two blue and two black pens. Two pens are chosen at random.

    a List the possible outcomes.

    b Write down the probability of choosing red and black pens.

4 Tom, Nicola and Matt each buy a drink. They either choose cola or lemonade.

    a Copy and complete the table.

    b What is the probability that Nicola and Matt choose different drinks?

Tom	Nicola	Matt
Cola	Cola	Lemonade

5 Two dice are rolled and the scores are added together. Copy and complete the sample space of scores.

	1	2	3	4	5	6
1	2	3				
2	3					

a What is the most likely total?

b What is the probability that the total is the following?

    i 2   **ii** 5   **iii** 1   **iv** 12

    v Even   **vi** Odd   **vii** 10, 11 or 12

    viii 6 or 8   **ix** Less than 4   **x** Less than or equal to 4

Extension Work

The scores on these two spinners are added to get a total score.

a Complete a sample space to show the total scores.

b What is the most likely total?

c What is the probability for each of the following totals?

    i 1   **ii** 3   **iii** 5   **iv** −2

    v −3   **vi** 0   **vii** Greater than 0   **viii** 2 or −2

Estimates of probability

In an experiment to test whether a dice is biased, the dice was rolled 120 times. These are the results.

Number on dice	1	2	3	4	5	6
Frequency	18	25	20	22	14	21

Do you think that the dice is biased?

Number 2 was rolled 25 times out of 120. So, an **estimate of the probability** of rolling number 2 is given by:

$$\frac{25}{120} = 0.208$$

The fraction $\frac{25}{120}$ is called the **estimate of the probability** or the **relative frequency**.

Relative frequency is an estimate of probability based on experimental data. The relative frequency may be the only way of estimating probability when events are not equally likely.

$$\text{Relative frequency} = \frac{\text{Number of successful trials}}{\text{Total number of trials}}$$

Example 9.4 ▷ Look again at the test results given opposite.

A dice is rolled 120 times. Here are the results.

Number on dice	1	2	3	4	5	6
Frequency	18	25	20	22	14	21

a Write down the relative frequency of a score of 6.

b How could you obtain a more accurate estimate than the relative frequency?

a Number 6 was rolled 21 times so the relative frequency is $\frac{21}{120}$.

b A more accurate estimate could be obtained by carrying out more trials.

Exercise 9C

1 A four-sided spinner was spun 100 times. Here are the results.

Number on spinner	1	2	3	4
Frequency	20	25	23	32

a What is the estimated probability of a score of 4?

b What is the estimated probability of an even score?

c Do you think from these results that the spinner is biased? Give a reason for your answer.

2 A drawing pin was thrown and the number of times that it landed point up was recorded at regular intervals. The results are shown in the table.

a Copy and complete the table for the estimated probabilities.

Number of throws	10	20	30	40	50
Number of times pin lands point up	6	13	20	24	32
Estimate of probability of landing point up	$\frac{3}{5}$				

b What is the best estimate of the probability of the pin landing point up?

3 A bag contains yellow and blue cubes. Cubes are picked from the bag, the colour recorded and the cubes replaced.

a Copy and complete the table for the relative frequencies for the number of times a blue cube is chosen.

Number of trials	10	25	50	100
Number of times blue cube chosen	3	8	15	28
Relative frequency	0.3			

b What is the best estimate of the probability of picking a blue cube from the bag?

In an experiment to test whether a dice is biased, the dice is rolled 120 times. These are the results.

Number on dice	1	2	3	4	5	6
Frequency	18	25	20	22	14	21

Number 2 was rolled 25 times out of 120. So, for example, you would expect it to be rolled 50 times out of 240. The expected number of successes can be calculated from the formula:

Expected number of successes = Relative frequency × Number of trials

Hence, in this case, the expected number of times number 2 is rolled is given by:

$$\frac{25}{120} \times 240 = 50$$

1   A four sided spinner was spun 100 times. Here are the results.

Number on spinner	1	2	3	4
Frequency	20	25	23	32

If the spinner was spun 500 times, how many times would you expect to get a score of 4?

2   A drawing pin was thrown and the number of times it landed point up was recorded at regular intervals. The results are shown in the table.

Number of throws	10	20	30	40	50
Number of times pin lands point up	6	13	20	24	32
Relative frequency of landing point up	0.6				

How many times would you expect the pin to land point up in 200 throws?

3   A bag contains yellow and blue cubes. Cubes are picked from the bag, and the cubes replaced. The results are shown in the table.

Number of trials	10	25	50	100
Number of times blue cube chosen	3	8	15	28
Relative frequency	0.3			

You are told that altogether there are 75 cubes in the bag. What is the best estimate of the number of blue cubes in the bag?

What you need to know for level 4

- How to extract information from tables and lists
- How to interpret a frequency diagram

What you need to know for level 5

- Understand and be able to use the probability scale from 0 to 1
- How to find and justify probabilities from equally likely events
- How to find probabilities based on experimental evidence

National Curriculum SATs questions

LEVEL 4

1 *2003 Paper 1*

A teacher has five number cards. She says:

'I am going to take a card at random.

Each card shows a different positive whole number.

It is certain that the card will show a number less than 10.

It is impossible that the card will show an even number.'

What numbers are on the cards?

2 *1996 Paper 2*

A machine sells sweets in five different colours:

red   green   orange   yellow   purple

You cannot choose which colour you get.

There is the same number of each colour in the machine.

Two boys want to buy a sweet each.

I don't like yellow ones or orange ones.

Ken

I like all of them.

Colin

a What is the probability that Ken will get a sweet that he likes?

b What is the probability that Colin will get a sweet that he likes?

c Draw an arrow on the scale to show the probability that Ken will get a sweet that he likes.

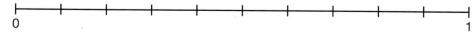

0   1

d Draw an arrow on the scale to show the probability that Colin will get a sweet that he likes.

0   1

e Mandy buys one sweet. The arrow on this scale shows the probability that Mandy gets a sweet that she likes.

Mandy

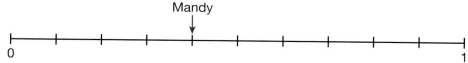

0   1

Write a sentence that could describe which sweets Mandy likes.

LEVEL 5

3 *1996 Paper 2*

Barry is doing an experiment. He drops 20 matchsticks at random onto a grid of parallel lines.

Barry does the experiment 10 times and records his results.
He wants to work out an estimate of probability.

Number of the 20 matchsticks which have fallen across a line

| 5 | 7 | 6 | 4 | 6 | 8 | 5 | 3 | 5 | 7 |

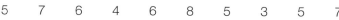
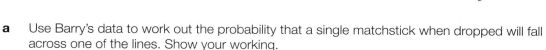

a Use Barry's data to work out the probability that a single matchstick when dropped will fall across one of the lines. Show your working.

b Barry continues the experiment until he has dropped the 20 matchsticks 60 times.

About how many matchsticks in total would you expect to fall across one of the lines? Show your working.

CHAPTER **10** Shape, Space and Measures **3**

This chapter is going to show you

- how to enlarge a shape by a scale factor
- how to recognise planes of symmetry in 3-D shapes
- how to use scale drawings

What you should already know

- Be able to recognise reflective symmetry in 2-D shapes
- How to draw plans
- How to use ratio
- Be able to plot coordinates in all four quadrants

Enlargements

The three transformations you have met so far (reflections, rotations and translations) do not change the size of the object. You are now going to look at a transformation that does change the size of an object. It is called **enlargement**. The illustration shows a picture which has been enlarged.

The diagram shows △ABC enlarged to give △A'B'C'.

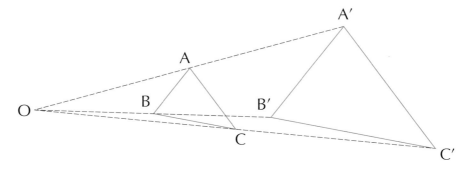

Each side of △A'B'C' is twice as long as the corresponding side of △ABC. Notice also that OA' = 2 × OA, OB' = 2 × OB and OC' = 2 × OC. That is, △ABC is enlarged by a **scale factor** of two about the **centre of enlargement**, O, to give the **image** △A'B'C'. The dashed lines are called the **guidelines** or **rays** for the enlargement.

To enlarge a shape, a **centre of enlargement** and a **scale factor** are needed.

Example 10.1

Enlarge the triangle XYZ by a scale factor of two about the centre of enlargement, O.

Draw rays OX, OY and OZ. Measure the length of each ray. Multiply each length by two. Then extend each ray to

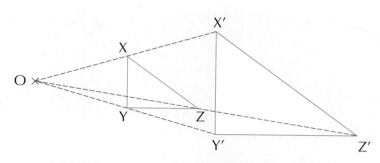

its new length measured from O and plot the points X', Y' and Z'. Join X', Y' and Z'. △X'Y'Z' is the enlargement of △XYZ by a scale factor of two about the centre of enlargement, O.

Example 10.2

The **object** rectangle ABCD on the coordinate grid shown has been enlarged by a scale factor of 3 about the origin, O, to give the **image** rectangle A'B'C'D'.

The coordinates of the object are: A(0, 2), B(3, 2), C(3, 1) and D(0, 1). The coordinates of the image are: A'(0, 6), B'(9, 6), C'(9, 3) and D'(0, 3).

Notice that when a shape is enlarged by a scale factor about the origin of a coordinate grid, the coordinates of the enlarged shape can be found by multiplying the coordinates of the original shape by the scale factor.

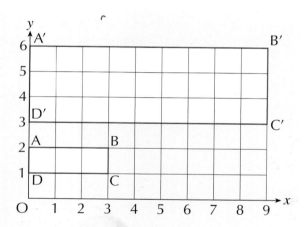

Exercise 10A

1 Draw copies of (or trace) the shapes below. Then enlarge each one by the given scale factor about the centre of enlargement O.

a Scale factor 2   **b** Scale factor 3   **c** Scale factor 2   **d** Scale factor 3

(Note: × is the centre of square)

2 Copy each diagram below on to centimetre-square paper. Then enlarge each one by the given scale factor about the origin O.

a

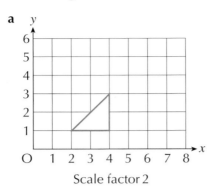

Scale factor 2

b

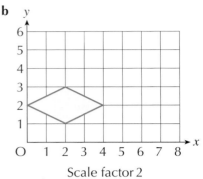

Scale factor 2

c

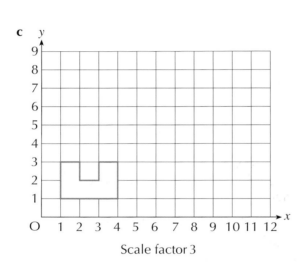

Scale factor 3

d

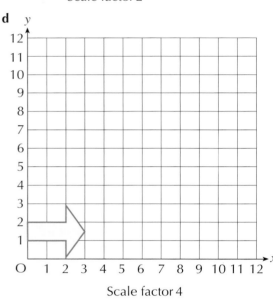

Scale factor 4

3 Draw axes for x and y from 0 to 10 on centimetre-square paper. Plot the points A(4, 6), B(5, 4), C(4, 1) and D(3, 4) and join them together to form the kite ABCD. Enlarge the kite by a scale factor of 2 about the point (1, 2).

4 Copy the diagram shown on to centimetre-square paper.

a Enlarge the square ABCD by a scale factor of two about the point (5, 5). Label the square A′B′C′D′. Write down the coordinates of A′, B′, C′ and D′.

b On the same grid, enlarge the square ABCD by a scale factor of three about the point (5, 5). Label the square A″B″C″D″. Write down the coordinates of A″, B″, C″ and D″.

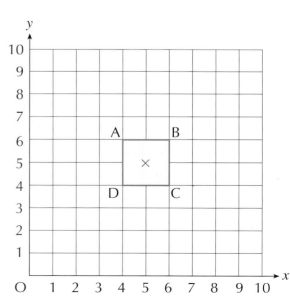

c On the same grid, enlarge the square ABCD by a scale factor of four about the point (5, 5). Label the square A‴B‴C‴D‴. Write down the coordinates of A‴, B‴, C‴ and D‴.

d What do you notice about the coordinate points that you have written down?

5 Copy the diagram shown on to centimetre-square paper.

a What is the scale factor of the enlargement?

b By adding suitable rays to your diagram, find the coordinates of the centre of enlargement.

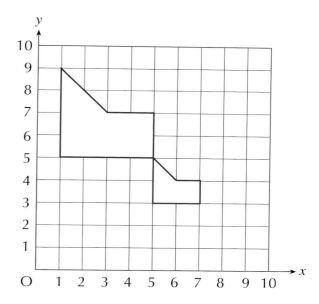

Extension Work

1 Working in pairs or groups, design a poster to show how the stick-man shown can be enlarged by different scale factors about any convenient centre of enlargement.

2 Use reference books or the Internet to explain how each of the following use enlargements.

a Slide projectors   **b** Telescopes   **c** Microscopes

3 Use ICT software, such as LOGO, to enlarge shapes by different scale factors and with different centres of enlargement.

3-D symmetry

You have already met reflective symmetry for 2-D shapes. As you know, some 2-D shapes have lines of symmetry. For example, a rectangle has two lines of symmetry and a regular hexagon has six lines of symmetry.

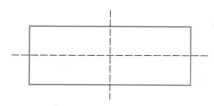

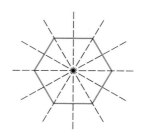

Some 3-D shapes, or solids, also have reflective symmetry.

The shape below can be cut exactly in half with the halves identical.

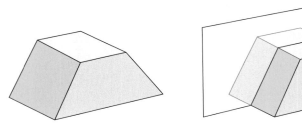

The mirror forms a **plane of symmetry** for the shape. A plane is a flat (2-D) surface. A plane of symmetry divides a 3-D shape into two identical halves.

Example 10.3 ▷ A cuboid has three planes of symmetry. That is, it can be sliced into halves in three different ways.

Each plane of symmetry is a rectangle.

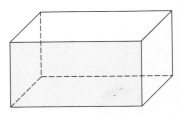

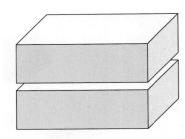

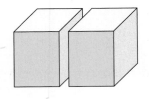

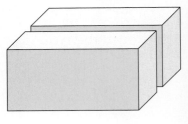

1 Which of the following 3-D objects have reflective symmetry?

a

b

c

d

e

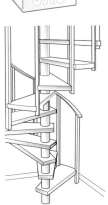

f

g

h

i

j

2 Write down the number of planes of symmetry for each of the following 3-D shapes.

a Cuboid with two square faces

b Cube

c Square-based pyramid

3 Write down the number of planes of symmetry for each of the following regular prisms.

a Triangular prism

b Hexagonal prism

c Octagonal prism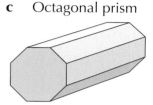

4 Draw sketches to show the different planes of symmetry for each of the following solids.

a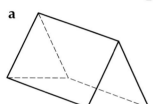

b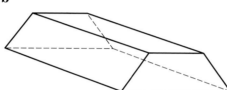

c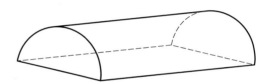

Extension Work

1 Draw sketches of some everyday objects which have one or more planes of symmetry. Below each sketch, write the number of planes of symmetry for the object.

2 Four cubes can be arranged to make the following different solids. Write down the number of planes of symmetry for each.

a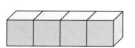

b

c

d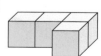

e

f

g

h

Using scale drawings

A **scale drawing** is a smaller (or sometimes larger) drawing of an actual object. The scale must always be clearly given by the side of or beneath the scale drawing.

Here you are going to be shown how to draw a shape to its full size from a scale drawing.

Example 10.4

The rectangle on the right has been drawn to scale.

The scale shows that each centimetre on the diagram represents 2 cm on the full-sized rectangle.

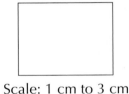

4 cm

1 cm

Scale: 1 cm to 2 cm

So, the length of the full-sized rectangle is
4×2 cm = 8 cm.

The width of the full-sized rectangle is 1×2 cm = 2 cm.

The rectangle can now be drawn with its actual measurements, as shown on the right.

8 cm

2 cm

Exercise 10C

1 The following rectangles are drawn to scale. Measure each of the sides. Then draw each rectangle to its full size.

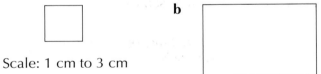

a

Scale: 1 cm to 3 cm

b

Scale: 1 cm to 2 cm

c

Scale: 1 cm to 2 cm

d

Scale: 1 cm to 3 cm

2 The following shapes are drawn to scale. Measure each of the sides. Then draw each shape to its full size.

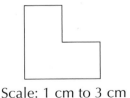

a

Scale: 1 cm to 3 cm

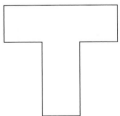

b

Scale: 1 cm to 2 cm

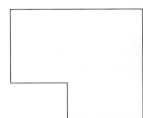

c

Scale: 1 cm to 2 cm

3 The following right-angled triangles are drawn to scale. Measure the vertical and horizontal sides of each of them. Then draw each triangle to its full size. Measure the length of the sloping side.

a

Scale: 1 cm to 2 cm

b

Scale: 1 cm to 3 cm

c

Scale: 1 cm to 4 cm

4 The shape on the right is drawn to scale. Measure the vertical and horizontal sides and draw the shape to its full size. Measure the length of the sloping side.

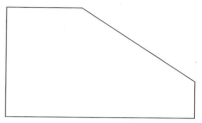

Scale: 1 cm to $1\frac{1}{2}$ cm

Scales written as ratios

Sometimes, particularly on plans and maps, a scale is written with mixed units. For example: 1 cm to 2 m, 5 cm to 1 km, 1 cm to 20 km.

These scales can also be given as ratios. This involves giving both parts of the ratio in the same unit. So, for example, the scale 1 cm to 2 m is first changed into centimetres, giving 1 cm to 200 cm. This can be expressed as the ratio 1 : 200. Notice that the ratio has no units.

Similarly, the scale 5 cm to 1 km can be changed into centimetres as 5 cm to 100 000 cm. This can be written as the ratio 5 : 100 000, which can be simplified to 1 : 20 000.

Write each of the following scales as a ratio.

1	1 cm to 1 m	**2**	1 cm to 5 m	**3**	4 cm to 1 m
4	2 cm to 5 m	**5**	1 cm to 1 km	**6**	4 cm to 1 km

What you need to know for level 4

- How to reflect a 2-D shape in a mirror line
- How to plot coordinates in the first quadrant

What you need to know for level 5

- How to plot coordinates in all four quadrants
- How to convert from one metric unit to another
- Solve problems using ratio

LEVEL 4

1 *2002 Paper 2*

Janet joins three points on a grid to make a triangle.
The coordinates of the points are:

    (0, 0) (1, 1) (2, 0)

The area of Janet's triangle is 1cm².

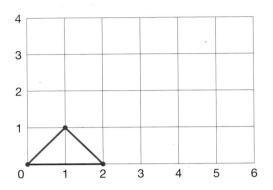

Dylan multiplies each of Janet's coordinates by 2.

Janet's coordinates	× 2	Dylan's coordinates
(0, 0)	—	(0, 0)
(1, 1)	—	(2, 2)
(2, 0)	—	(4, 0)

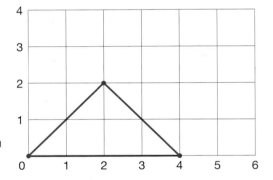

a What is the area of Dylan's triangle?

b Copy Janet's coordinates and multiply each of them by 3.

Janet's coordinates	× 3	New coordinates
(0, 0)	—	(…,…)
(1, 1)	—	(…,…)
(2, 0)	—	(…,…)

Plot the three points with the new coordinates on a copy of the grid below. Join them up to make a triangle.

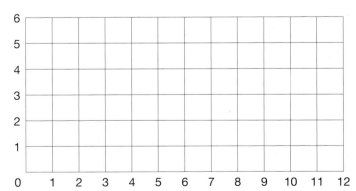

c What is the area of your triangle?

Nazir multiplies each of Janet's coordinates by another number. He plots two of the points, (0, 0) and (10, 0), and joins them up.

d Plot Nazir's third point on a copy of the grid below.

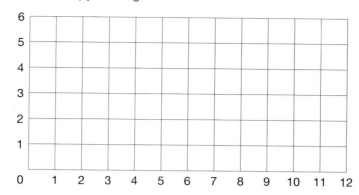

e By what number did Nazir multiply Janet's coordinates?

2 *1999 Paper 2*

This cuboid is made from four small cubes.

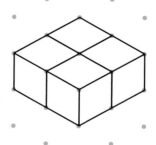

a On a copy of the isometric grid below, draw a cuboid which is twice as high, twice as long and twice as wide.

b Graham made this cuboid from three small cubes.

Mohinder wants to make a cuboid which is twice as high, twice as long and twice as wide as Graham's cuboid. How many small cubes will Mohinder need altogether?

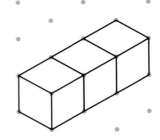

LEVEL 5

3 *2002 Paper 2*

I have a paper circle. Then I cut a sector from the circle. It makes this net.

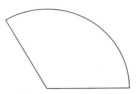

Which 3-D shape below could I make with my net?

A   B   C   D   E

This chapter is going to show you

○ how to combine like terms
○ how to expand brackets
○ how to rearrange formulae
○ how to draw a graph from the equation $y + ax + b = 0$

What you should already know

○ Be able to use indices to represent squares
○ How to substitute values into formulae
○ How to plot points on a grid

Like terms

Like terms are multiples of the same letter, or of the same combination of letters. Also, they can be the same power of the same letter or the same powers of the same combination of letters. For example:

$x, 4x, \frac{1}{2}x, -3x$ Like terms which are multiples of x

$5ab, 8ab, \frac{1}{2}ab, -2ab$ Like terms which are multiples of ab

$y^2, 3y^2, \frac{1}{4}y^2, -4y^2$ Like terms which are multiples of y^2

The multiples are called **coefficients**. So, in the above examples, 1, 4, $\frac{1}{2}$, –3, 5, 8, –2, 3, $\frac{1}{4}$ and –4 are coefficients.

Only like terms can be added or subtracted to simplify an expression. For example :

$3ab + 2ab$ simplifies to $5ab$

$8x^2 - 5x^2$ simplifies to $3x^2$

Unlike terms cannot be simplified by addition or subtraction. For example:

$9a + 5a + 10b - 4b = 14a + 6b$

The expression $14a + 6b$ cannot be simplified because $14a$ and $6b$ are unlike terms.

Simplifying an expression means making it shorter by combining its terms where possible. This usually involves two steps:

● Collect the like terms into groups of the same sort.
● Combine each group of like terms, and simplify.

Example 11.1 Simplify $7x + 3y + 4x + 5t + 6y + 8$.

First step is to collect the like terms together:

$7x + 4x + 3y + 6y + 5t + 8$

Second step is to combine the like terms:

$11x + 9y + 5t + 8$

This is the original expression's simplest form.

Example 11.2

Simplify $5a^2 + d^2 + 3a^2 - 4d^2 + 5e - 7$.

First step is to collect the like terms together:
$$5a^2 + 3a^2 + d^2 - 4d^2 + 5e - 7$$

Second step is to combine the like terms:
$$8a^2 - 3d^2 + 5e - 7$$

This is the original expression's simplest form.

Example 11.3

Simplify $5a^2 + 4d - 3a^2 - 9d$.

Collecting together its like terms gives:
$$5a^2 - 3a^2 + 4d - 9d$$

Combining them gives:
$$2a^2 - 5d \text{ which is the original expression's simplest form.}$$

Exercise 11A

1 Simplify each of these.

a $3x + 4x$ **b** $4a + 3a$ **c** $7t + t$ **d** $4y + y + 3y$

e $8m - 2m$ **f** $7k - 4k$ **g** $5n - n$ **h** $3p - 7p$

2 Simplify each of these.

a $6m + m + 3m$ **b** $2y + 4y + y$ **c** $6t + 2t + t$ **d** $5p + 2p + 4p$

e $6n + 2n + 5n$ **f** $5p + 3p + p$ **g** $4t - t + 3t$ **h** $4e - 2e + 5e$

i $7k + 2k - 3k$ **j** $6h + h - 2h$ **k** $9m - 3m - m$ **l** $5t + 3t - 2t$

3 Write down the perimeter, P, of each of the following shapes.

a   **b**   **c** 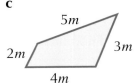   **d** 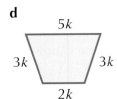   **e** 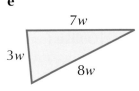   **f**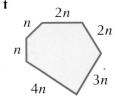

4 Simplify each of the following expressions.

a $4b + 3 + b$ **b** $5x + 6 + 2x$ **c** $q + 3 + 5q$ **d** $5k + 2k + 7$

e $4x + 5 - 2x$ **f** $7k + 3 - k$ **g** $5p + 1 - 3p$ **h** $8d + 2 - 5d$

i $6m - 2 - 4m$ **j** $5t - 3 - 3t$ **k** $5w - 7 - 2w$ **l** $6g - 5 - 2g$

m $2t + k + 5t$ **n** $4x + 3y + 5x$ **p** $3k + 2g + 4k$ **q** $5h + w + 3w$

r $7t + 3p - 4t$ **s** $8n + 3t - 6n$ **t** $p + 5q - 4q$ **u** $4n + p - 2n$

5 Simplify each of the following expressions.

a $3t + 4g + 6t + 3g$ **b** $5x + y + 3x + 4y$ **c** $3m + k + 4m + 3k$

d $6x + 4y - 3x + 2y$ **e** $7m + p - 3m + 2p$ **f** $4n + 3t - n + 2t$

g $7k + 4g - 3k - g$ **h** $6d + 5b - 3d - 2b$ **i** $5q + 4p - 3q - p$

j $5g - k + 3g + 4k$ **k** $6x - 2y + x + 3y$ **l** $5d - 2e - 8d + e$

1 Joe said: 'Two prime numbers can never add to gether to make another prime number.' Is Joe correct? Explain your answer.

2 Can you make any prime numbers as the sum of three prime numbers? Explain your answer.

Expanding brackets

When a number or a letter is next to brackets everything in the brackets has to be multiplied by that number or letter if the brackets are to be removed.

This process is called **expanding the brackets** or **multiplying out**.

Example 11.4 ▷ Expand $3(4h + 5)$.

Multiply each term by 3:
$$3 \times 4h + 3 \times 5$$
which gives: $12h + 15$

Example 11.5 ▷ Expand $-2(6m - 5p - 4)$.

Multiply each term by -2:
$$-2 \times 6m - 2 \times -5p - 2 \times -4$$
which gives: $-12m + 10p + 8$
Move the negative term to obtain: $10p - 12m + 8$

Example 11.6 ▷ Expand $m(4p + 2)$.

Multiply each term by m:
$$m \times 4p + m \times 2$$
which gives: $4mp + 2m$

Example 11.7 ▷ Expand $t(5t - 3)$.

Multiply each term by t:
$$t \times 5t - t \times 3$$
which gives: $5t^2 + 3t$

1 Multiply out each of the following brackets.

a	$2(m + 3)$	**b**	$3(k - 4)$	**c**	$3(a + 2)$	**d**	$5(3 - p)$
e	$2(3x + 4)$	**f**	$5(2x + 3)$	**g**	$4(2t - 1)$	**h**	$5(4m + 7)$
i	$3(2x + 1)$	**j**	$4(3k - 2)$	**k**	$2(5b + 3)$	**l**	$7(2 - 4m)$
m	$8(3 + p)$	**n**	$5(4 - t)$	**p**	$6(w - g)$	**q**	$8(p + t)$
r	$9(2k - 6)$	**s**	$5(2m + w)$	**t**	$3(3t - 2d)$	**u**	$2(3x - 4y)$

2 Write down an expression for the area, A, of each of the following rectangles.

a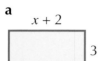
$x + 2$; 3

b
2 ; $2x + 5$

c
$3m + 4$; 5

d
$5k + p$; 7

e
$3t + 2$; 4

f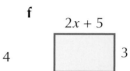
$2x + 5$; 3

3 Multiply out each of the following.

a	$x(y + 2)$	**b**	$m(3a + 2)$	**c**	$k(2p + 4)$	**d**	$n(6m + 3)$
e	$t(5 + 4q)$	**f**	$g(3 + 4h)$	**g**	$h(7 + 5g)$	**h**	$k(3 + 2d)$
i	$a(4b - 3)$	**j**	$c(5 - 4d)$	**k**	$f(2 - 3m)$	**l**	$b(5 - 4a)$
m	$d(5a + 3)$	**n**	$e(7f + 3)$	**p**	$y(3x + 2)$	**q**	$p(2q + 5)$
r	$q(3 - 4p)$	**s**	$t(6 - 3s)$	**t**	$w(8 - 5k)$	**u**	$n(3 - 2m)$

4 Write down an expression for the area, A, of each of the following rectangles.

a
$x + 5$; y

b
$2x + 3$; m

c
$6 + 3a$; d

d
$2a + 3$; k

e
$3 + 5y$; n

f
$5p + 6$; q

5 Multiply out each of the following.

a	$x(x + 2)$	**b**	$m(3m + 2)$	**c**	$k(4k + 1)$	**d**	$n(4n + 3)$
e	$t(6 + 2t)$	**f**	$g(1 + 4g)$	**g**	$h(3 + 5h)$	**h**	$d(2 + 3d)$
i	$a(5a - 2)$	**j**	$c(3 - 4c)$	**k**	$t(5 - 3t)$	**l**	$b(7 - 4b)$
m	$d(8d + 7a)$	**n**	$e(5e + 3)$	**p**	$y(2x + 3y)$	**q**	$p(5 + 4p)$
r	$q(7q - 5)$	**s**	$t(2t - 5)$	**t**	$w(3w - 4)$	**u**	$n(8n - 5)$

6 Write down an expression for the area, A, of each of the following rectangles.

a
$4m + 3$; m

b
$6 + 3t$; t

c
$3k + 1$; k

d
$4 + 3x$; x

e
$2g + 7$; g

f
$3 + 2n$; n

a   Write down any three-digit number whose first and last digits have a difference of more than one (for example, 472 or 513).

b   Reverse the order of the digits (for the examples above, 274 and 315).

c   Subtract the smaller number from the larger number.

d   Reverse the digits of the answer to part **c** and add this number to the answer to part **c**.

e   Multiply the answer by one million.

f   Subtract 733 361 573.
   - Then, under each 2 in your answer, write the letter P.
   - Under each 3, write the letter L.
   - Under each 4, write the letter R.
   - Under each 5, write the letter O.
   - Under each 6, write the letter F.
   - Under each 7, write the letter A.
   - Under each 8, write the letter I.

g   Now read your letters backwards.

Expanding and simplifying

Sometimes, two brackets have to be expanded and the results added together.

You have met both of these processes before. Now you are going to put them together. Follow through Examples 11.8 to 11.10.

Example 11.8   Expand and simplify $4(5 + 2y) + 2(5y - 6)$.

Multiply out both brackets, to obtain: $20 + 8y + 10y - 12$

Bring like terms together, which gives: $8y + 10y + 20 - 12$

Simplify to obtain: $18y + 8$

Example 11.9   Expand and simplify $4(2u + 3i) - 2(u - 2i)$.

Multiply out both brackets, to obtain: $8u + 12i - 2u + 4i$

Bring like terms together, which gives: $8u - 2u + 12i + 4i$

Simplify to obtain: $6u + 16i$

Example 11.10   Expand and simplify $x(3x + 4) - x(x - 5)$.

Multiply out both brackets, to obtain: $3x^2 + 4x - x^2 + 5x$

Bring like terms together, which gives: $3x^2 - x^2 + 4x + 5x$

Simplify to obtain: $2x^2 + 9x$

1 Expand and simplify each of the following expressions.

a $2(3x + 4) + 3(x + 2)$

b $4(2k + 3) + 3(4k + 7)$

c $5(2t + 3) + 2(3t + 4)$

d $4(3q + 2) + 3(2q + 1)$

e $6(3h + 2) + 4(2h - 1)$

f $5(6 + 3f) + 2(2 - 3f)$

g $4(3 - 2y) + 3(2 + 3y)$

h $6(2t - 5) + 3(5t - 2)$

2 Expand and simplify each of the following expressions.

a $3(2x + 5) - 2(x + 3)$

b $5(2k + 4) - 2(4k + 1)$

c $6(3t + 4) - 3(2t + 5)$

d $7(2q + 3) - 4(3q + 4)$

e $8(2h + 5) - 3(4h - 2)$

f $7(w + 4) - 3(2w - 3)$

g $5(4x - 3) - 3(3x - 2)$

h $9(2t - 3) - 2(6t - 3)$

3 Expand and simplify each of the following expressions.

a $x(2x + 5) + x(4x + 3)$

b $p(3p + 4) + p(2p + 1)$

c $k(5k + 3) + k(2k + 4)$

d $d(3d + 5) + d(2d + 3)$

e $n(5n + 6) + n(3n - 5)$

f $f(5f + 3) + f(3f - 2)$

g $p(p - 5) + p(2p - 4)$

h $y(5y - 2) + y(4y - 3)$

4 Expand and simplify each of the following expressions.

a $x(8x + 5) - x(4x + 1)$

b $p(5p + 4) - p(2p + 1)$

c $k(4k + 4) - k(2k + 3)$

d $d(3d + 7) - d(2d + 4)$

e $n(7n + 5) - n(3n - 2)$

f $f(6f + 5) - f(3f - 4)$

g $p(3p - 1) - p(p - 5)$

h $y(4y - 3) - y(2y - 7)$

Extension Work

a Write down any three different, whole numbers smaller than ten. For example: 2, 5 and 8.

b Add up these three numbers. Call this total x.

c Make all the six possible two-digit numbers using these three different numbers. For example: 25, 28, 52, 58, 82 and 85.

d Add up all six numbers. Call this total y.

e Divide y by x and write down the answer.

f Repeat this for other sets of three different whole numbers smaller than ten. What do you notice?

Changing the subject of a formula

Look at the formula $E = 5t + 3$.

The formula states the value of the variable E, in terms of the variable t and 3. E is called the **subject** of the formula.

Often, a formula has to be rearranged to make one of the other **variables** in it the subject. This is done in a similar way to solving equations, by adding, subtracting, multiplying or dividing both sides of the formula by the same quantity in order to leave that variable on its own as the subject of the formula.

Example 11.11

Change $E = 5t + 3$, to make t the subject.

The formula needs altering so that t is on its own.

Subtract 3 from both sides, which gives: $E - 3 = 5t + 3 - 3$

This simplifies to: $E - 3 = 5t$

Divide both sides by 5, to obtain: $\dfrac{E - 3}{5} = \dfrac{5t}{5}$

which simplifies to: $\dfrac{E - 3}{5} = t$

Turn round the new formula, so that t is on the left-hand side, to give

$$t = \frac{E - 3}{5}$$

Example 11.12

Rewrite $N = 5(2m - p)$ to express m in terms of N and P.

First, expand the bracket, to obtain: $N = 10m - 5p$

Add $5p$ to both sides of the equation, which gives: $N + 5p = 10m - 5p + 5p$

which simplifies to: $N + 5p = 10m$

Divide both sides by 10 and simplify, to obtain: $\dfrac{N + 5p}{10} = m$

Turn the new formula round so that m is on the left-hand side, to give

$$m = \frac{N + 5p}{10}$$

Example 11.13 ▷

Make V the subject of the formula $D = \dfrac{M}{V}$

Multiply both sides by V, to give:

$$DV = \frac{M}{\cancel{V}} \times \cancel{V}$$

$$DV = M$$

Now divide both sides by D, to give:

$$\frac{\cancel{D}V}{\cancel{D}} = \frac{M}{D}$$

$$V = \frac{M}{D}$$

Exercise 11D

1 Rewrite each of the following formulae as indicated.

a $T = m + p$ Express m in terms of T and p.
b $Q = p + t$ Express t in terms of Q and p.
c $N = w - q$ Express w in terms of N and q.
d $B = ak$ Express a in terms of B and k.
e $V = at$ Express a in terms of V and t.
f $P = 2a + 2b$ Express a in terms of P and b.
g $P = 5m + 4n$ Express m in terms of P and n.
h $A = 3(m + n)$ Express m in terms of A and n.
i $W = 5(p + 2)$ Express p in terms of W.

2 Rewrite each of the following formulae as indicated.

a $C = \pi D$ Make D the subject of the formula.
b $A = 6(k + h)$ Make k the subject of the formula.
c $S = r(h + 7)$ Make h the subject of the formula.
d $V = \pi r^2 h$ Make h the subject of the formula.
e $S = 2t + 3$ Make t the subject of the formula.

3 $D = 4m + 7$

i   Find D when $m = 8$.   ii   Make m the subject of the formula.
iii Find m when $D = 27$.

4 $P = b + 4k$

i   Find P when $b = 8$ and $k = 5$.   ii   Make k the subject of the formula.
iii Find k when $P = 27$ and $b = 3$.

5 $u = 3m - p$

i   Find u when $m = 7$ and $p = 2$.
ii   Make m the subject of the formula.
iii Find m when $u = 27$ and $p = 6$.

6 $T = 8m + 5n$

    i   Find T when $m = 4$ and $n = 9$.

    ii   Make n the subject of the formula.

    iii Find n when $T = 67$ and $m = 4$.

7 Use the formula $K = 5m + 3h$ to find the value of h when $m = 8$ and $K = 61$.

8 The average speed, S mph, of a car travelling a distance of D miles, in time t hours, is given by the formula:

$$S = \frac{D}{t}$$

  a **i**   Change the formula to make D the subject.

       ii   Use your formula to find the distance travelled when driving a car at an average speed of 68 mph for $2\frac{1}{2}$ hours.

  b **i**   Change the formula to make t the subject.

       ii   Use your formula to find the time taken to travel 385 miles when driving a car at an average speed of 55 mph.

Extension Work

- Choose any three-digit number with all its digits the same: for example, 555. Call this number y.

- Add together all the digits. Write this total down. Call it x. For the example above: $5 + 5 + 5 = 15$, so $x = 15$.

- Divide y by x and write down the answer.

- Try this with another three-digit number (with all its digits the same). What do you notice?

- Can you find out why this happens?

Graphs from equations $y + Ax + B = 0$

You have already met the linear equation of the form $y = mx + c$ which gives a straight-line graph. This is the same equation here in the form $y + Ax + B = 0$. When a graph is drawn from an equation in this form, the result is still a straight line.

To create the graph:

- Rearrange the equation into the form $y = mx + c$.
- Use a table of three or four suitable values of x which give y.
- Draw a pair of axes (preferably on squared graph paper) and plot the points.
- Draw a straight-line graph through all the points.

Example 11.14

Draw the graph of $y - 5x + 4 = 0$.

First, rearrange the equation:

$y - 5x + 4 = 0$

Add $5x$ to both sides which gives:

$y + 4 = 5x$

Subtract 4 from both sides to obtain:

$y = 5x - 4$

Next, construct a table of values.

x	0	1	2	3
y	−4	1	6	11

Now, draw a pair of axes, plot the points and draw a straight line through all the points.

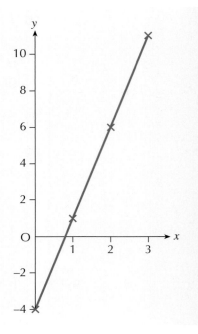

1 Rearrange each of the following to make y the subject.

a $y - x + 1 = 0$ **b** $y - 2x + 1 = 0$ **c** $y - 2x + 3 = 0$

d $y - 3x - 4 = 0$ **e** $y - 4x - 3 = 0$ **f** $y - 5x - 1 = 0$

2 Copy and complete the following values for each of the given equations. (Rearrange each equation to make y the subject before you substitute.)

a $y - x + 1 = 0$

x	0	1	2	3
y				

b $y - x + 2 = 0$

x	0	1	2	3
y				

c $y - 2x - 3 = 0$

x	0	1	2	3
y				

d $y - 4x - 1 = 0$

x	0	1	2	3
y				

i   Copy and complete the following tables of values for the given equations. (Rearrange each equation to make y the subject before you substitute.)

ii Use each table to draw the graph of its equation, using the axes as shown on the right.

a $y - 2x - 1 = 0$

x	0	1	2	3
y				

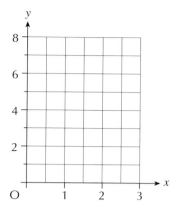

b $y - 3x - 1 = 0$

x	0	1	2	3
y				

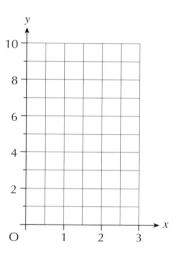

c $y - 2x - 5 = 0$

x	0	1	2	3
y				

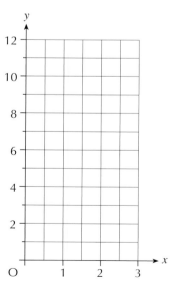

4 Draw a pair of axes as shown on the right.

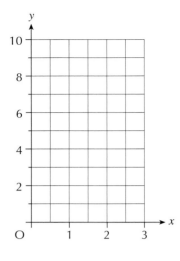

Draw the graph of each of the following equations on the same pair of axes as given.

i $y - x - 1 = 0$

ii $y - x - 2 = 0$

iii $y - x - 3 = 0$

iv $y - x - 4 = 0$

Comment on the similarities and the differences between the graphs.

5 Investigate the similarities and the differences between the following graphs.

a $y - 2x - 1 = 0$ **b** $y - 2x - 2 = 0$

c $y - 2x - 3 = 0$ **d** $y - 2x - 4 = 0$

Extension Work

1 Investigate the similarities and the differences between the following graphs.

a $y + x - 5 = 0$ **b** $y + x - 1 = 0$

c $y + x - 4 = 0$ **d** $y + x - 3 = 0$

2 Investigate the similarities and the differences between the following graphs.

a $y + 2x - 5 = 0$ **b** $y + 2x - 1 = 0$

c $y + 2x - 4 = 0$ **d** $y + 2x - 3 = 0$

What you need to know for level 4

○ How to substitute values into expressions

○ Be able to recognise the use of the square indices

What you need to know for level 5

○ How to combine like terms

○ How to expand a simple bracket

○ How to plot a few points on a grid and draw a graph

LEVEL 5

1   *2000 Paper 1*

Write each expression in its simplest form.

  a $7 + 2t + 3t$

  b $b + 7 + 2b + 10$

  c $(3d + 5) + (d - 2)$

  d $3m - (-m)$

2   *Adapted from 2002 Paper 1*

  a   Simplify $(6n + 8) - (2n + 3)$.

  b   What expression should be in the bracket if $2(?) = 6n + 8$?

CHAPTER 12 · Solving problems and Revision

This chapter is going to give you practice in SATs questions about

- Fractions, percentages and decimals
- The four rules, ratios and directed numbers
- Algebra – the basic rules and solving linear equations
- Algebra – graphs
- Shape, space and measures
- Handling data

Number 1 – Fractions, percentages and decimals

Exercise 12A   **Do not use a calculator for the first eight questions.**

1 How much of each shape is shaded? Tick the correct box.

a

More than half ☐
Half ☐
Less than half ☐

b

More than a third ☐
A third ☐
Less than a third ☐

c

More than a quarter ☐
A quarter ☐
Less than a quarter ☐

2 a About 33% of this rectangle is dotted.

About what **percentage** is   **i** striped   **ii** plain?

b About $\frac{1}{8}$ of this rectangle is red.

About what **percentage** is   **i** blue   **ii** white?

3 Identify which four of the following numbers are equivalent.

$$0.06 \qquad 60\% \qquad 0.60 \qquad \frac{6}{100} \qquad \frac{3}{5} \qquad 6\% \qquad \frac{6}{10}$$

4 If $\frac{5}{12}$ of the members of a youth club are girls, what fraction are boys?

5 This is the sign at an airport's long-stay car park.

How much would it cost to park at the airport for 9 days?

FLYPARK

£6.50 per day or
£42.50 for a full week.

6 **a** A Scots pine tree is 4.35 metres tall. A larch pine is 84 cm taller. How tall is the larch pine?

b From Barnsley to Sheffield via the motorway is 26.45 km. If you go via the ordinary roads it is 3.8 km shorter. How far is it from Barnsley to Sheffield via the ordinary roads?

7 Calculate the following, giving your answers as fractions.

a $\frac{3}{5} + \frac{1}{3}$
b $\frac{5}{9} - \frac{1}{6}$
c $2\frac{3}{4} + 1\frac{2}{5}$

8 The following method can be used to work out 12% of 320:

```
10% of 320 =  32
 1% of 320 =   3.2
 1% of 320 =   3.2
12% of 320 =  38.4
```

Use a similar method or a method of your own to work out 28% of 480.

You may use a calculator for the rest of the exercise.

9 **a** Add 356 to half of 422.
b Take a quarter of 156 from 200.

10 Some bathroom scales measure in stones and pounds, whilst others measure in kilograms. One way to change from stones and pounds to kilograms is shown below.

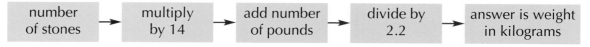

number of stones → multiply by 14 → add number of pounds → divide by 2.2 → answer is weight in kilograms

Convert 11 stone 10 pounds to kilograms.

11 The train fare for an adult from Sheffield to London is £97. A child's fare is 35% less than this. How much is a child's fare?

12 Jack's Jackets is having a sale:

Calculate the sale price of a jacket that is normally priced at £42.60.

JACK'S JACKETS

15% off all jackets

13 This table shows the populations (in **thousands**) of the eight largest towns in the United Kingdom in 1991 and in 2001. It also shows the percentage change in the populations of the towns over that 10 year period.

Town	London	Birmingham	Leeds	Glasgow	Sheffield	Liverpool	Manchester	Bristol
1991	6 800	1 007	717	660	529	481	439	407
2001	7 200	1 017	731	692	531	456		423
% change	5.9%	1%	2.0%	4.8%	0.3%	−5.2%	−3.2%	

a How many more people lived in Leeds than Sheffield in 2001?

b Calculate the population of Manchester in 2001.

c Calculate the percentage change in the population of Bristol over the 10 years.

Number 2 – The four rules, ratios and directed numbers

Exercise 12B

Do not use a calculator for the first eight questions.

1 a Add together 143 and 328. **b** Subtract 183 from 562.

  c Multiply 66 by 4. **d** Divide 132 by 6.

2 a Fill in the missing numbers on the number lines below.

i 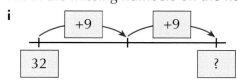 ii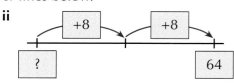

b On this number line, both steps are the same size. How big is each step?

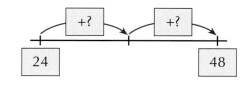

3 a Copy each number sequence below and put in the correct sign, '<', '=' or '>', to make each one true.

  i −6 ... −2 ii 8 − 6 ... −2 iii 7 − 7 ... 5 − 8

b Here is a list of numbers.

  −8   −6   −4   −2   0   1   3   5

  i Choose two numbers from the list that have a total of −1.

  ii What is the total of all the numbers in the list?

  iii Choose two different numbers from the list to make the lowest possible value when put in these boxes:

  ☐ − ☐ = ...

4 Write a number at the end of each equation to make it correct.

    a 27 + 53 = 17 + ...   **b** 76 − 28 = 66 − ...

    c 50 × 17 = 5 × ...   **d** 400 ÷ 10 = 4000 ÷ ...

5 Use +, −, × or ÷ to make each calculation correct.

    For example, for 3 ... 7 = 2 ... 5, you could insert '+' and '×' to give 3 + 7 = 2 × 5.

    a 9 ... 6 = 20 ... 5   **b** 15 ... 3 = 4 ... 3

    c 5 ... 2 = 15 ... 5   **d** 8 ... 4 = 4 ... 2

6 A teacher has 32 students in her class. She decides to buy each student a pen for Christmas, costing 98p. How much will it cost her altogether?

7 Litter bins cost £29 each. A school has a budget of £500 to spend on bins. How many bins can the school afford?

8 Alf and Bert are paid £48 for doing a job. They decide to share the money in the ratio 3 : 5. How much does Alf get?

You may use a calculator for the rest of the exercise.

9 Copy and fill in the missing numbers.

    a 783 − ? = 348   **b** ? − 234 = 621   **c** 34 × ? = 918

    d 4629 = ? + 68   **e** ? ÷ 33 = 19   **f** 568 = 879 − ?

10 a Brenda buys fish, chips and mushy peas.

      i How much does she pay?

      ii How much change does she get from a £10 note?

    b Abdul has £2.15. He wants a burger and a chip butty. Does he have enough money?

PRICE LIST	
Fish	£1.65
Chips	£0.80
Mushy Peas	£0.45
Burger	£1.25
Bread Bun	£0.30

11 Give the missing number for each of these number chains.

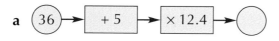

    a (36) → [+ 5] → [× 12.4] → ◯   **b** (36) → [− 5] → [÷ 12.4] → ◯

    c (36) → [×] → (450)   **d** (364) → [÷] → (35)

12 A car company wants to move 700 cars by rail. Each train can carry 48 cars.

    a How many trains will be needed to move the 700 cars?

    b Each train costs £3745. What is the total cost of the trains?

    c What is the **cost per car** of transporting them by train?

13 a A bus travels 234 miles in 4 hours and 30 minutes. What is the average speed of the bus?

    b A car travels 280 miles at an average speed of 60 miles per hour. How long was the car travelling for? Give your answer in hours and minutes.

Algebra 1 – Basic rules and solving linear equations

Do not use a calculator for this exercise.

1 A box of pencils contains x pencils and costs £y.

   a How many pencils are there in 6 boxes?

   b How much do 5 boxes cost?

   c Which expression represents the cost of x boxes of pencils?

      i £$(x + y)$ **ii** £xy

2 Solve the following equations:

   a $x + 5 = 7$ **b** $3x = 12$ **c** $x - 6 = 10$

3 This advertisement shows how much a plumber charges.

   a How much would Ivor charge for a job that lasted 2 hours?

   b If Ivor charged £110 for a job, how long did it last?

> **Ivor Wrench**
> **Emergency plumber**
> £30 callout charge
> plus £20 per hour

4 **a** What is the next coordinate in the list below?

      (2, 1),   (4, 3),   (6, 5),   (8, 7),   …

   b Explain why the coordinate (29, 28) could not be part of this sequence.

5 a, b and c represent the weights in kilograms of three children, Ali, Billie and Charlie.

   a Match each of the following algebraic expressions with one of the statements below.

      $a = 30$ $b = 2a$

      $b + c = 75$ $\dfrac{a + b + c}{3} = 35$

   Statement 1: Billie weighs twice as much as Ali.

   Statement 2: The mean weight of all three children is 35 kilograms.

   Statement 3: Ali weighs 30 kilograms.

   Statement 4: Billie and Charlie weigh 75 kilograms together.

   b Use the information to work out Billie's weight and Charlie's weight.

6 Look at the algebraic expressions on the cards below.

$2 \times n$ $n^3 \div n$ $n + n$ $0.5n$ $n \div 2$

$n \times n$ $3n - n$ $n \times 2$ $6n \div 3$

    a Which two expressions will always give the same answer as $\frac{n}{2}$?

    b Which two expressions will always give the same answer as n^2?

    c Five of the expressions are the same as $2n$. Write an expression of your own that is the same as $2n$.

7 The diagram shows a square with sides of length $(n + 4)$ cm.

The square has been split into four smaller rectangles. The area of one rectangle is shown.

    a Fill in the three missing areas with a number or an algebraic expression.

    b Write down an expression for the total area of the square.

	n	4
n	......	$4n$
4	......	......

8 Expand the brackets and simplify the following expressions if possible.

    a $4(x - 5)$ **b** $3(2x + 1) + 5x$ **c** $3(x - 2) + 2(x + 4)$

    d $5(3x + 4) + 2(x - 2)$ **e** $4(2x + 1) - 3(x - 6)$

9 **a** When $x = 4$ and $y = 6$ work out the value of each of the three expressions below.

        i $3x + 9$ **ii** $4x - y$ **iii** $2(3x + 2y + 1)$

    b Solve the equations below to find the value of z in each case.

        i $5z + 9 = 24$ **ii** $\frac{z - 8}{2} = 7$ **iii** $5z + 9 = 3z + 7$

10 Two friends, Selma and Khalid are revising algebra.

Selma says 'I am thinking of a number. If you multiply it by 6 and add 3 you get an answer of 12.'

Khalid says 'I am thinking of a number. If you multiply it by 3 and subtract 6 you get the same answer as adding the number to 7.'

    a Call Selma's number x and form an equation. Then solve the equation.

    b Call Khalid's number y and form an equation. Then solve the equation.

Algebra 2 – Graphs

Do not use a calculator for this exercise.

You will need graph paper or centimetre-squared paper.

For any graphs you are asked to draw, axes the size of the ones in the fourth question will be big enough.

1 **a** The point M is halfway between points A and C. What are the coordinates of M?

b Shape ABCD is a square. What are the coordinates of the point D?

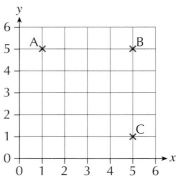

2 The graph shows points A, B, and C.

a What are the coordinates of A and B?

b ABCD makes a rectangle. What are the coordinates of D?

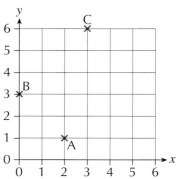

3 The graph shows the line $y = 3$.

Copy the diagram and draw on it the graphs of:

a $y = 5$ **b** $x = 4$

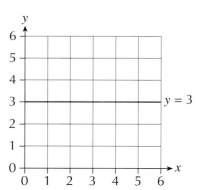

4 Each of the lines labelled l_1, l_2, l_3 and l_4 has one of the equations in the list below. Match each line to its equation.

a $y = 2$ **b** $y = x$

c $x = -3$ **d** $y = -x$

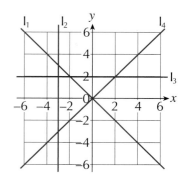

5 Draw and label each of the following graphs.

    a $y = 2x + 1$ **b** $y = \frac{1}{2}x - 1$ **c** $x + y = 3$

6 Does the point (20, 30) lie on the line $y = 2x - 10$? Explain your answer.

7 The distance–time graph shows the journey of a jogger on a 5-mile run. At one point she stopped to admire the view and at another point she ran up a steep hill.

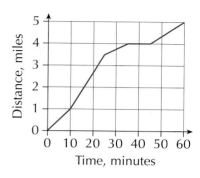

    a For how long did she stop to admire the view?

    b What distance into her run was the start of the hill?

8 In a house, the hot water tank automatically refills with cold water whenever hot water is taken out. The heating system then heats the water to a pre-set temperature.

Dad always has a shower in the morning. Mum always has a bath and the two children get up so late that all they do is wash their hands and faces.

The graph shows the temperature of the water in the hot water tank between 7 AM and 9 AM one morning.

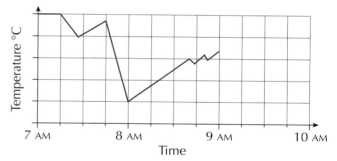

    a At what time did Dad have his shower?

    b At what time did Mum have her bath?

    c At what time did the first child wash?

    d Gran likes to have as hot a bath as possible, once everyone else has left the house at 9 AM. Estimate at what time the water will be back to its maximum temperature.

9 For every point on the graph of $x + y = 6$, the x- and y-coordinates add up to 6. Which of the following points lie on the line?

    a **i** (3, –3)   **ii** (6, 0)   **iii** (–7, –1)   **iv** (–1, 7)

    b On a grid draw the graph of $x + y = 6$.

10 The graph shows the line $y = 2x + 2$

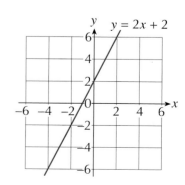

    a Copy the graph and draw and label the line $y = 2x - 1$ on the same axes.

    b Draw and label the line $y = x + 2$ on the same axes.

    c Write down the coordinates of the point where the graphs $y = 2x - 1$ and $y = x + 2$ intersect.

Shape, space and measures

Do not use a calculator for Questions 1 to 7.

You will find squared paper useful for Questions 5 and 12.

1 For each of the following shapes write down:

    i   the number of lines of symmetry.

    ii the order of rotational symmetry.

2 In parts **a** to **c** write down the name of the quadrilateral being described.

    a   It has 4 right angles. It has 2 lines of symmetry.

    b   It has 1 pair of equal angles. It has 2 pairs of equal sides.

    c   It has no lines of symmetry. It has rotational symmetry of order 2.

    d   Complete the following for a Rhombus.

        i   It has ...... equal sides.

        ii It has ...... lines of symmetry.

        iii It has rotational symmetry of order ....

3 **a**   What is the area of this rectangle?

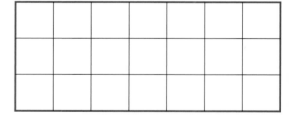

    b   The rectangle is cut into four triangles as shown. What is the area of one of the larger triangles?

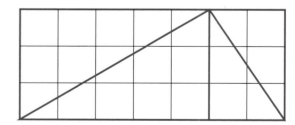

c The four triangles are put together to form a kite. What is the area of the kite?

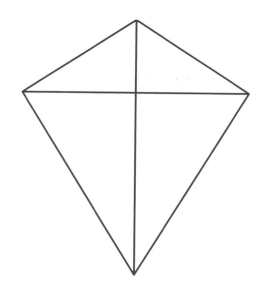

4 a Describe angles A–E in the diagram using the correct words chosen from this list:

      Acute   **Obtuse**

      Reflex   **Right-angled**

b Is angle A bigger, smaller or the same size as angle C? Explain your answer.

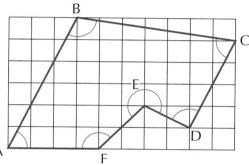

5 Copy each of the following diagrams and shade in more circles so that the dotted lines are lines of symmetry. You may find squared paper helpful.

a

  ◯ ◯ ◯ ┆ ◯ ◯ ◯
  ● ◯ ◯ ┆ ◯ ◯ ◯
  ◯ ● ◯ ┆ ● ◯ ◯
  ◯ ◯ ● ┆ ● ● ●
  ◯ ◯ ● ┆ ◯ ◯ ◯
  ◯ ◯ ◯ ┆ ◯ ◯ ◯

b

  ◉ ◯ ◯ ◯ ◯ ◯
  ◯ ◉ ◯ ◯ ◯ ◯
  ◯ ◯ ● ◯ ◯ ◯
  ◯ ● ● ◉ ◯ ◯
  ◯ ● ● ◯ ◉ ◯
  ◯ ● ◯ ◯ ◯ ◉

c

  ◯ ◯ ◯ ┆ ● ◯ ◯
  ◯ ◯ ◯ ┆ ● ● ◯
  ◯ ◯ ◯ ┆ ● ◯ ●
  ─ ─ ─ ┼ ─ ─ ─
  ◯ ◯ ◯ ┆ ◯ ◯ ◯
  ◯ ◯ ◯ ┆ ◯ ◯ ◯
  ◯ ◯ ◯ ┆ ◯ ◯ ◯

6 a Copy and complete the two-way table to show the symmetries of each of the shapes shown. Shape A has been done for you.

		Number of lines of symmetry				
		0	**1**	**2**	**3**	**4**
Order of rotational symmetry	**1**		A			
	2					
	3					
	4					

b Name a quadrilateral that has two lines of symmetry and rotational symmetry of order 2.

7 Find the values of angles *a*, *b* and *c* in this diagram. The lines marked with arrows are parallel.

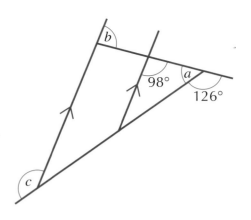

You may use a calculator for the rest of this exercise.

8 a A rectangle measures 24 cm by 12 cm. What is its area?

b The rectangle is folded in half several times until it measures 6 cm by 3 cm. How many times was it folded?

c What is the ratio of the **areas** of the original rectangle and the smaller rectangle? Give your answer in its simplest form.

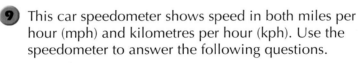

9 This car speedometer shows speed in both miles per hour (mph) and kilometres per hour (kph). Use the speedometer to answer the following questions.

a How many kilometres are equivalent to 50 miles?

b Is someone travelling at 100 kph breaking the speed limit of 70 mph? Justify your answer.

c About how many miles is 150 kilometres? Explain your answer.

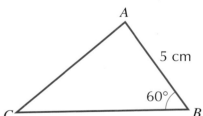
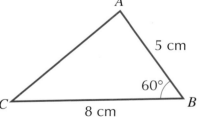

10 a Make an accurate construction of this triangle.

b Measure the angle at A.

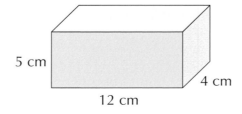

11 The diagram shows a cuboid and a triangular prism. Both solids have the same volume. Use this information to calculate the length of the prism.

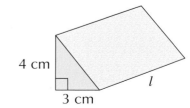

Handling data

You do not need to use a calculator for this exercise.

1 This bar chart shows the favourite pets of 80 students.

a How many students chose a rabbit as their favourite pet?

b How many more students preferred a cat to a horse?

c What is the difference between the number of students who chose the most popular pet and those who chose the least popular?

Favourite Pets

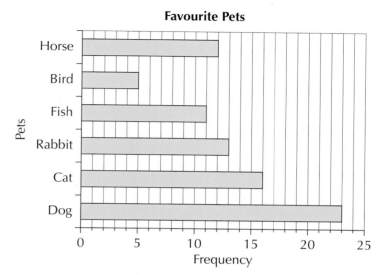

2 This table shows the types and colours of vehicles passing a school between 9am and 10am.

	Red	Black	White	Blue
Lorries	2	6	0	3
Vans	3	1	7	2
Cars	6	5	9	8

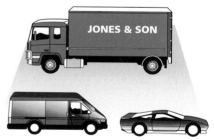

JONES & SON

a How many white vans passed the school?

b How many lorries passed the school altogether?

c How many more blue vehicles than red vehicles passed the school?

3 This is the calendar for the first two months of 2004.

JANUARY					
Mon		5	12	19	26
Tue		6	13	20	27
Wed		7	14	21	28
Thu	1	8	15	22	29
Fri	2	9	16	23	30
Sat	3	10	17	24	31
Sun	4	11	18	25	

FEBRUARY					
Mon		2	9	16	23
Tue		3	10	17	24
Wed		4	11	18	25
Thu		5	12	19	26
Fri		6	13	20	27
Sat		7	14	21	28
Sun	1	8	15	22	29

a The Disney marathon in Florida is on the second Sunday in January. What date is this?

b There are 5 days the same (Sundays) in February. This only happens every four years. Explain why.

c Mr. Henry is going to Florida for a holiday. He arrives on the 22nd of January and leaves on the 11th of February. How many **nights** will he be in Florida?

4 a Zeenat rolls an ordinary six-sided dice. What is the probability that the dice shows an even number?

b Zeenat now rolls the dice and tosses a coin. One way that the dice and the coin could land is to show a head and a score of 1. This can be written as (H, 1).

Copy and complete the list below to show all the possible outcomes.

(H, 1), (H, 2), …

c Zeenat rolls the dice and it shows a score of 6. She rolls the dice again. What is the probability that the dice shows a score of 6 this time?

5 Two four-sided dice, each numbered 1, 2, 3, 4 are thrown. The table shows all the possible total scores.

a When the two dice are thrown what is the probability that the total score is a square number?

b When the two dice are thrown what is the probability that the score is greater than 5?

c i Draw a table to show all the possible products if the numbers on each of the dice are multiplied together.

ii What is the probability that the product is a number less than 17?

Score on first dice

Score on second dice	1	2	3	4
1	2	3	4	5
2	3	4	5	6
3	4	5	6	7
4	5	6	7	8

6 A bag contains only red and blue marbles. A marble is to be taken from the bag at random.

It is twice as likely that the marble will be red as blue. Give a possible number of red and blue marbles in the bag.

7 Hakim has 5 cards.

a What is the mode of the numbers on the cards?

b What is the median of the numbers on the cards?

c What is the mean of the numbers on the cards?

8 Look at the three different spinners, P, Q and R, below.

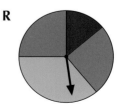

a Which spinner has the greatest chance of landing on red?

b Which spinner has an evens chance of landing on blue?

c Which two spinners have an equal chance of landing on green?

9 Paul's marks for his last nine maths homeworks are:

9, 3, 5, 4, 4, 7, 5, 8, 6

a What is the range of his marks?

b What is the median mark?

c After checking the final homework, Paul realised that his teacher did not mark one of the questions. Once this had been marked, Paul's mark increased from 6 to 8.

Say whether each of the statements, **i**, **ii** and **iii** are true, false or if it is not possible to say.

Explain your answers.
i The mode of the marks has increased.
ii The median mark has increased.
iii The mean mark has increased.

10 The probability that a ball taken at random from a bag is black is 0.7. What is the probability that a ball taken at random from the same bag is **not** black?

11 Lee and Alex are planning a survey of what students at their school prefer to do at the local entertainment complex, where there is a cinema, a bowling alley, a games arcade and a disco.

a Alex decides to give out a questionnaire to all the students in a Year 7 tutor group. Explain why this may not give reliable results for the survey.

b Lee decides to include this question in his questionnaire:

How many times in a week do you go to the entertainment complex?

Never ☐   1–2 times ☐   2–5 times ☐   every day ☐

Explain why this is not a good question.

This chapter is going to show you

- some of the statistical techniques you have met before
- how to make a hypothesis
- how to carry out a handling data investigation

What you should already know

- How to carry out a survey
- How to write a questionnaire
- How to collect data
- How to construct and interpret two-way tables
- How to construct and interpret frequency diagrams
- How to interpret scatter graphs
- How to calculate averages
- How to calculate a range
- How to construct and interpret a stem-and-leaf diagram

Statistical techniques

This lesson will remind you of the statistical techniques that you have met before. In the next lesson you will be using these to carry out a handling data project.

The following tables show the vocabulary you should know before you start an investigation.

Handling Data vocabulary

Collecting data

	Definition	Example
Questionnaire	A set of questions used to collect information from people	Here is an example of a poor question: How old are you? ☐ 0–10　☐ 10–20 ☐ 20–30　☐ over 30 It is poor because the categories overlap, so that both 10 and 20 are in two response sections.
Population	The set of people or objects being investigated	A school with 1000 students
Sample	Part of the whole population being used for analysis	50 students picked from the 1000 in a school
Survey	The collection of data from a sample of the population	Investigating the favourite colour of students in a school by asking 50 students
Census	The collection of data from an entire population	Investigating the favourite colour of students in a school by asking *every* student in the school

	Definition	Example
Data collection sheet or Observation sheet	A form for recording results	Favourite colours of 50 students:
Tally	A means of recording data quickly	Blue 卌 卌 Red 卌 卌 卌 III Green 卌 卌 IIII Other 卌 III
Raw data	Data which has not been sorted or analysed	Ages of 10 students: 12, 14, 13, 11, 12, 12, 15, 13, 11, 12
Primary data	Data that *you* have collected, usually by observation, surveys or experiments	Colours of cars on your street
Secondary data	Data collected by someone else and then used by you	Acceleration times of different cars

Two-way table — A table for combining two sets of data

	Ford	Vauxhall	Peugeot
Red	3	5	2
Blue	1	0	4
Green	2	0	1

Frequency table — A table showing the quantities of different items or values

Weight of parcels *W* (kg)	Number of parcels (frequency)
$0 < W \leq 1$	5
$1 < W \leq 2$	7
$W > 2$	3

Frequency diagram — A diagram showing the quantities of different items or values

BAR CHART

PIE CHART

LINE GRAPH

	Definition	Example
Stem-and-leaf diagram	A way of grouping data, in order	**Recorded speeds of 17 cars** 2 | 3 7 7 8 9 9 3 | 1 2 3 5 5 5 7 9 4 | 2 2 5 Key: 2 | 3 means 23 miles per hour
Population pyramid	A statistical diagram often used for comparing large sets of data	 **Age distribution in France (2000)**
Scatter graph or scatter diagram	A graph to compare two sets of data	

Processing data

	Definition	Example
Mode	The value that occurs *most* often	Find the mode, median, mean and range of this set of data 23, 17, 25, 19, 17, 23, 21, 23
Median	The *middle* value when the data is written in order (or the average of the middle two values)	Sorting the data into order, smallest first, gives: 17, 17, 19, 21, 23, 23, 23, 25 Mode = 23
Mean	The sum of all the values divided by the number of items of data	Median = $\dfrac{21 + 23}{2} = 22$ Mean = $\dfrac{17 + 17 + 19 + 21 + 23 + 23 + 23 + 25}{8} = 21$
Range	The difference between the largest and smallest values	Range = 25 − 17 = 8

1 Criticise each of the following questions that were used in a questionnaire about travelling to school.

a How do you travel to school?

☐ Walk   ☐ Bus   ☐ Car

b How long does your journey take?

☐ 0 – 5 minutes   ☐ 5 – 10 minutes

☐ 10 – 15 minutes   ☐ 15 – 20 minutes

c What time do you usually set off to school?

☐ Before 8.00 am   ☐ 8.00 am – 8.15 am

☐ 8.15 am – 8.30 am   ☐ Other

2 Below are the times taken (*T* seconds) by 20 students to run 100 metres.

Boys	13.1	14.0	17.9	15.2	15.9	17.5	13.9	21.3	15.5	17.6
Girls	15.3	17.8	16.3	18.1	19.2	21.4	13.5	18.2	18.4	13.6

a Copy and complete the two-way table to show the frequencies.

	Boys		Girls	
	Tally	Frequency	Tally	Frequency
$12 \leq T < 14$	I I	2	I I	2
$14 \leq T < 16$				
$16 \leq T < 18$				
$18 \leq T < 20$				
$20 \leq T < 22$				

b Which is the modal class for the boys?

c Which is the modal class for the girls?

3 19 students take a test. The total marks were shown on the stem-and-leaf diagram.

```
0 | 5 6 8 9
1 | 0 1 1 2 2 4 4 5 6 6 7 8 9 9
2 | 0
```

Key: 0 | 6 means 6

a Write down the lowest and highest scores.

b State the range of the marks.

c Work out the median mark.

d How many students scored 15 or more in the test?

4 Look at the population pyramid for France in the year 2000 on page 178.

   a   Are there more males or females aged over 70? Explain your answer.

   b   Which age group is the largest for males?

   c   Which age group under 50 is the smallest for females?

5 Calculate the mode, the median and the mean for each set of data below.

   a   1, 1, 1, 4, 8, 17, 50

   b   2, 5, 11, 5, 8, 7, 6, 1, 4

   c   £2.50, £4.50, £2, £3, £4.50, £2.50, £3, £4.50, £3.50, £4, £3.50

   d   18, 18, 19, 21, 24, 25

6 A school quiz team is made up of students from four different classes. The table shows the number of students in the team from each class.

Class	Number of students
A	4
B	3
C	8
D	5

   a   Represent this information in a pie chart.

   b   Holly says, 'The percentage of students chosen from class C is double the percentage chosen from class A.' Explain why this might not be true.

Extension Work

It was estimated that there were 58 836 700 people living in the UK in mid 2001. This was an increase of 1.4 million people (2.4 per cent) since 1991.

The graph shows the population (in thousands) of the UK between 1991 and 2001. Explain why it may be misleading.

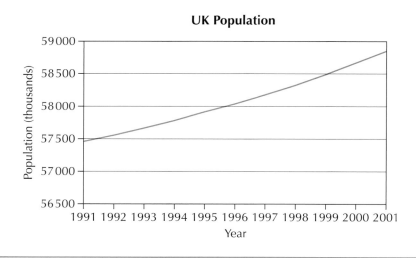

UK Population

A handling data project

In this section you are going to plan and write a handling data investigation. Look at the handling data cycle below. This shows the basic steps in an investigation.

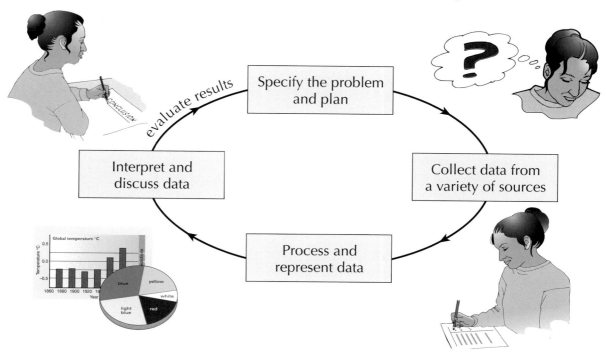

More detail is given about each step below. Follow this checklist when doing your investigation and writing your report.

- **Specify the problem and plan**
  - statement of problem or topic to investigate
  - hypothesis stating what you think the investigation will show
  - how you will choose your sample and sample size
  - any practical problems you foresee
  - how you will obtain your data, possibly including how to avoid bias

- **Collect data from a variety of sources**
  - follow initial plan and use a suitable data-collection sheet

- **Process and represent data**
  - analysis of your results using appropriate statistical calculations and diagrams

- **Interpret and discuss data**
  - comparison of results with your original hypothesis
  - list of any factors which might have affected your results and how you could overcome these in future
  - a final conclusion

Exercise 13B

In small groups investigate one of the following topics.

1. Compare people's hand-span with their shoe size.

2 Compare the reaction times of two different groups of people, for example girls and boys.

3 Investigate the ability of people to estimate the lengths of lines (straight or curved) and to estimate the size of angles.

4 Compare the word lengths in a newspaper with those in a magazine, or compare the word lengths in two different newspapers.

5 Choose your own investigation.

Choose one of the following tasks.

1   Working individually, write a report of your investigation using the checklist. Look again at the limitations of your investigation and think how you could overcome these, for example by increasing your sample size or choosing your sample using a different method.

2   In your small group, create a display which can be used as part of a presentation to show the other groups in your class how you carried out your investigation and what results you obtained. Look again at the limitations of your investigation and think how you could overcome these, for example by increasing your sample size or choosing your sample using a different method.

3   If you have completed your report, then consider a different problem from the list in **Exercise 13B**. Write a plan of how you would investigate it, including how to overcome any problems encountered in your first project.

Shape, Space and Measures 4

This chapter is going to show you

- some of the methods already met when dealing with shapes
- how to carry out a shape and space investigation
- how to carry out a symmetry investigation

What you should already know

- How to find the area of 2-D shapes
- How to find the surface area and the volume of a cuboid
- How to use reflective and rotational symmetry

Shape and space revision

Before starting an investigation into shape and space, you must be familiar with all the formulae and terms which you have met so far.

This section provides a checklist before you start your investigation.

Perimeter and area

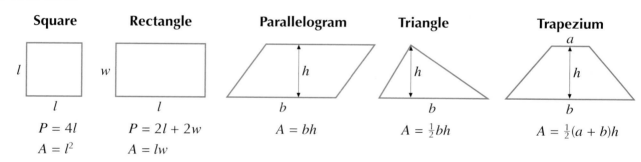

| Square | Rectangle | Parallelogram | Triangle | Trapezium |

$$P = 4l$$
$$A = l^2$$

$$P = 2l + 2w$$
$$A = lw$$

$$A = bh$$

$$A = \tfrac{1}{2}bh$$

$$A = \tfrac{1}{2}(a + b)h$$

Remember that the metric units for perimeter are the same as for length: millimetres (mm), centimetres (cm) and metres (m).

Remember that the metric units for area are: square millimetres (mm²), square centimetres (cm²) and square metres (m²).

Volume and surface area

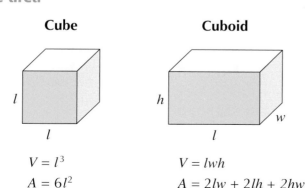

Cube

Cuboid

$$V = l^3$$
$$A = 6l^2$$

$$V = lwh$$
$$A = 2lw + 2lh + 2hw$$

Remember that the metric units for volume are: cubic millimetres (mm³), cubic centimetres (cm³) and cubic metres (m³).

1 Find **i** the perimeter and **ii** the area of each of the following rectangles.

a

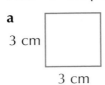

3 cm

3 cm

b

4 cm

5 cm

c

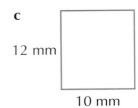

12 mm

10 mm

d

5 m

12 m

2 Find the area of each of the following triangles.

a

2 cm

4 cm

b

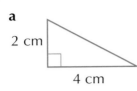

8 cm

5 cm

c

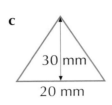

30 mm

20 mm

d

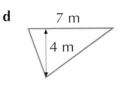

7 m

4 m

3 Find the area of each of the following shapes.

a

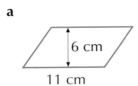

6 cm

11 cm

b

12 cm

8 cm

c

6 m

4 m

3 m

d

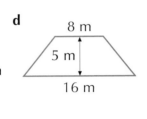

8 m

5 m

16 m

4 Find **i** the surface area and **ii** the volume of each of the following cuboids.

a

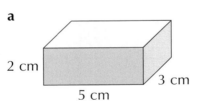

2 cm

5 cm

3 cm

b

5 cm

5 cm

5 cm

c

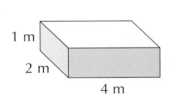

1 m

2 m

4 m

5 Calculate the area of the square drawn on the centimetre grid.

A formula to find the area of a kite is given here.
The lengths of the two diagonals of the kite are AC = a
and BD = b. The formula for the area of the kite is:

$$A = \frac{ab}{2}$$

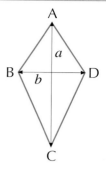

Use the formula to calculate the area of each of the following kites:

1

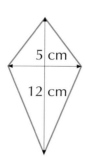

5 cm

12 cm

2

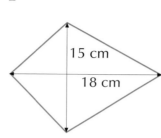

15 cm

18 cm

3

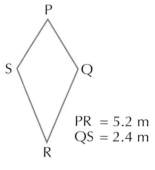

PR = 5.2 m
QS = 2.4 m

Shape and space investigations

When undertaking an investigation, you should carry out the following:

- Draw some easy examples first, making all diagrams clear with all measurements shown.
- Put your results in a table with suitable headings.
- Look for any patterns among the entries in the table.
- Describe and explain any patterns you spot.
- Try to find a rule or formula to explain each pattern.
- Try another example to see whether your rule or formula does work.
- Summarise your results with a conclusion.
- If possible, extend the investigation by introducing different questions.

Exercise 14B

Working in pairs or small groups, investigate one of the following.

1 Investigate whether the perimeter and the area of a square can have the same value. Extend the problem by looking at rectangles.

2 For the growing squares on the grid below, investigate the ratio of the length of a side to the perimeter and the ratio of the length of a side to the area.

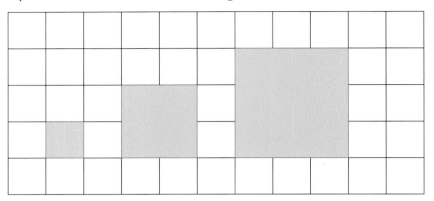

3 The shapes below are drawn on a 1 cm grid of dots.

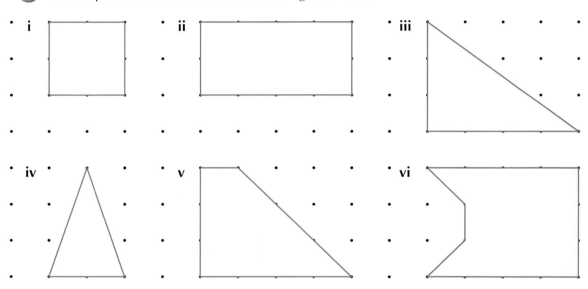

Shape	Number of dots on perimeter of shape	Number of dots inside shape	Area of shape (cm²)
i			
ii			
iii			
iv			
v			
vi			

a Copy and complete the table for each shape.

b Find a formula that connects the number of dots on the perimeter P, the number of dots inside I and the area A of each shape.

c Check your formula by drawing different shapes on a 1 cm grid of dots.

4 The diagram below represents a 6 × 2 snooker table with a pocket at each corner, A, B, C and D.

A snooker ball is hit from the corner at A at an angle of 45° and carries on bouncing off the sides of the table until it goes down one of the pockets.

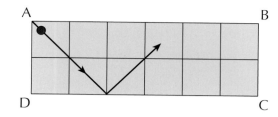

a How many times does the ball bounce off the sides before it goes down a pocket?

b Down which pocket does the ball go?

c Investigate for different sizes of snooker tables.

Symmetry revision

Before starting an investigation into symmetry, you must be familiar with the terms which you have met so far.

This section provides a checklist before you start your investigation.

There are two types of symmetry: **reflection symmetry** and **rotational symmetry**.

Some 2-D shapes have both types of symmetry, while some have only one type.

All 2-D shapes have rotational symmetry of order 1 or more.

Reflection symmetry

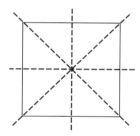

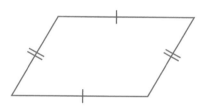

A square has 4 lines of symmetry   A parallelogram has no lines of symmetry

Remember that tracing paper or a mirror can be used to find the lines of symmetry of a shape.

Rotational symmetry

A 2-D shape has rotational symmetry when it can be rotated about a point to look exactly the same in its new position.

The **order of rotational symmetry** is the number of different positions in which the shape looks the same when rotated about the point.

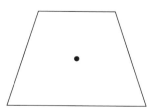

A square has rotational symmetry   This trapezium has rotational symmetry
of order 4   of order 1

Remember that tracing paper can be used to find the order of rotational symmetry of a shape.

Planes of symmetry

A **plane of symmetry** divides a 3-D shape into two identical parts. Each part is a reflection of the other in the plane of symmetry.

A cuboid has three planes of symmetry, as shown below.

Each plane of symmetry is a rectangle.

Exercise 14C

1. Copy each of these shapes and draw its lines of symmetry. Write below each shape the number of lines of symmetry it has.

   a   b    c   d   e

2. Write down the number of lines of symmetry for each of the following shapes.

   a    b    c   d

3. Copy each of the following diagrams and write the order of rotational symmetry below each one.

   a    b 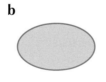   c   d    e

4. Write down the order of rotational symmetry for each of the following shapes.

   a    b 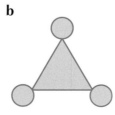   c    d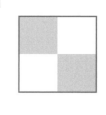

5 Write down the number of planes of symmetry for each of the following 3-D letters.

a   b 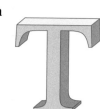   c   d

Symmetry investigations

When undertaking a symmetry investigation, you should carry out the following:

- Draw some easy examples first, showing any lines of symmetry and/or stating the order of rotational symmetry on the diagrams.
- Explain anything you notice from the diagrams.
- Describe and explain any patterns which you spot.
- Summarise your results with a conclusion.
- If possible, extend the investigation by introducing different questions.

Exercise 14D

Working in pairs or small groups, investigate one of the following.

1 Three squares are shaded on the 3×3 tile shown so that the tile has one line of symmetry.

     a Investigate the line symmetry of the tile when three squares are shaded.

     b Investigate the line symmetry when different numbers of squares are shaded.

Extend the problem by looking at different sizes of tiles.

2 Pentominoes are shapes made from five squares which touch edge to edge. For example:

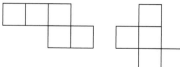

Investigate line symmetry and rotational symmetry for different pentominoes.

Extend the problem by looking at hexominoes. These are shapes made from six squares which touch edge to edge.

3 In how many ways will the T-shape fit inside the 3 × 3 grid?

Investigate the number of ways the T-shape will fit inside a 1 cm square grid of any size.

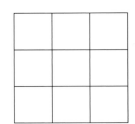

4 The **symmetry number** for a 3-D solid is the number of ways the solid can be placed through a 2-D outline of the solid.

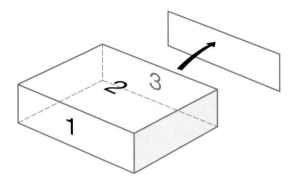

For example, the outline of a cuboid is a rectangle and the cuboid can be 'posted' (so that it fits exactly) through the rectangle in four different ways. These are:

    side 3 first, with side 2 facing up (shown above)
    side 3 first, with 2 facing down
    side 1 first, with 2 facing up
    side 1 first, with 2 facing down

So, the symmetry number for a cuboid is 4.

Investigate the symmetry number for other 3-D solids.

Revision of probability

Make sure that you are familiar with the vocabulary to do with probability which is listed in the table below.

Probability vocabulary

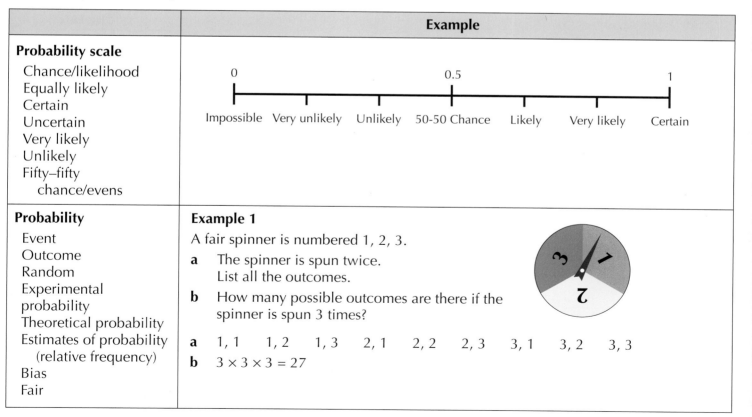

	Example
Probability scale Chance/likelihood Equally likely Certain Uncertain Very likely Unlikely Fifty–fifty chance/evens	0 0.5 1 Impossible Very unlikely Unlikely 50-50 Chance Likely Very likely Certain
Probability Event Outcome Random Experimental probability Theoretical probability Estimates of probability (relative frequency) Bias Fair	**Example 1** A fair spinner is numbered 1, 2, 3. **a** The spinner is spun twice. List all the outcomes. **b** How many possible outcomes are there if the spinner is spun 3 times? **a** 1, 1 1, 2 1, 3 2, 1 2, 2 2, 3 3, 1 3, 2 3, 3 **b** $3 \times 3 \times 3 = 27$

	Example
Probability *(continued)*	**Example 2** A six-sided dice is rolled 60 times. It lands on a 6 fifteen times. **a** What is the experimental probability of landing on a 6? **b** Do you think the dice is fair? **a** $\dfrac{15}{60} = \dfrac{1}{4}$ **b** No, because the experimental probability and the theoretical probability are different.

Probability diagrams
  Sample
  Sample space
	Example 3
	A coin is thrown and a dice is rolled.
	
	a Draw a sample space diagram.
	b Write down the probability of getting a head and a 6.
	
	a
	<table><tr><td colspan="2"></td><td colspan="6">**Dice**</td></tr><tr><td colspan="2"></td><td>1</td><td>2</td><td>3</td><td>4</td><td>5</td><td>6</td></tr><tr><td rowspan="2">**Coin**</td><td>Head</td><td>H,1</td><td>H,2</td><td>H,3</td><td>H,4</td><td>H,5</td><td>H,6</td></tr><tr><td>Tail</td><td>T,1</td><td>T,2</td><td>T,3</td><td>T,4</td><td>T,5</td><td>T,6</td></tr></table>
	b $\dfrac{1}{12}$

Events
  Exhaustive
  Independent
  Mutually exclusive
	Example 4
	In a raffle there are 100 tickets, coloured blue, green or yellow. The table shows the number of tickets of each colour.
	
	a What is the probability of picking a blue ticket?
	b What is the probability of picking a yellow ticket?
	c What is the probability of picking a blue or green ticket?
	d What is the probability of picking a ticket that is not green?
	
	a $\dfrac{1}{2}$
	
	b $\dfrac{3}{10}$
	
	c $\dfrac{7}{10}$
	
	d $1 - \dfrac{1}{5} = \dfrac{4}{5}$
	
	| Ticket colour
		Number of tickets

Blue	50
Green	20
Yellow	30	
Probability notation P(Event)	$P(\text{Green}) = \dfrac{1}{5}$

1 Ten cards are numbered 1 to 10. A card is picked at random. Work out the probability of picking:

  a the number 5
  b an even number
  c a number greater than 8
  d a number less than or equal to 4

2 Two coins are thrown.

  a How many different outcomes are there?
  b Work out the probability of getting no heads.
  c Work out the probability of getting two heads.
  d Work out the probability of getting exactly one head.

3 Matthew is either late, on time or early for school. The table shows his record over 10 days.

late	on time	early
1	3	6

Use the table to estimate the probability that on one day he is:
  a late
  b on time
  c early
  d not late

4 A group of 50 students are told to draw two straight lines on a piece of paper. Seven students draw parallel lines, twelve draw perpendicular lines and the rest draw lines which are neither parallel nor perpendicular.

Use these results to estimate the probability that a student chosen at random has:
  a drawn parallel lines
  b drawn perpendicular lines
  c drawn lines that are neither parallel nor perpendicular.

5 A five-sided spinner is spun 50 times. Here are the results.

Number on spinner	1	2	3	4	5
Frequency	8	11	10	6	15

  a Write down the experimental probability of the spinner landing on the number 4.
  b Write down the theoretical probability of a fair, five-sided spinner landing on the number 4.
  c Compare the experimental and theoretical probabilities and say whether you think the spinner is fair.

1   State whether each of the following pairs of events are independent or not independent. Explain your answers.

    a   Rolling a dice and getting a 6;
        Rolling the dice a second time and getting a 6.

    b   Picking out a winning raffle ticket;
        Picking out a second raffle ticket.

    c   It raining in London on Monday;
        It raining in London on Tuesday.

2   State whether each of the following pairs of outcomes are mutually exclusive or not mutually exclusive. Explain your answers.

    a   An ordinary, six-sided dice landing on an even number;
        The dice landing on a prime number.

    b   Two coins being thrown and getting at least one head;
        The two coins being thrown and getting two tails.

    c   Two coins being thrown and getting at least one tail;
        The two coins being thrown and getting two tails.

3   State whether each of the following outcomes are exhaustive or not exhaustive. Explain your answers.

    a   A dice landing on an odd number;
        The dice landing on a multiple of 2.

    b   A spinner numbered 1, 2, 3, 4, 5 landing on a number greater than 3;
        The spinner landing on a number less than 3.

    c   A spinner numbered 1, 2, 3, 4, 5 landing on a number greater than 2;
        The spinner landing on a number less than 4.

4   The probability that Sam is late for work is 0.1.

    a   What is the probability that he is not late for work?

    b   How many times would you expect him to be late over 50 days?

A probability investigation

Look again at the handling data cycle.

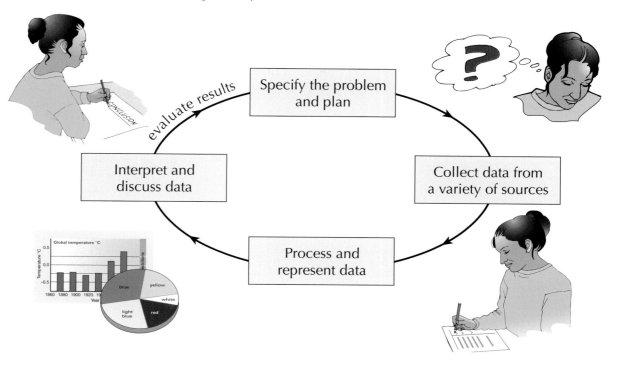

Use the handling data cycle to help you when completing your probability investigation. More detail is given about each step below.

- **Specify the problem and plan**
  - statement of problem or topic to investigate
  - hypothesis stating what you think the investigation will show
  - how you will choose your sample and sample size
  - any practical problems you foresee
  - how you will obtain your data, possibly including how to avoid bias

- **Collect data from a variety of sources**
  - follow initial plan and use a suitable data-collection sheet

- **Process and represent data**
  - analysis of your results using appropriate statistical calculations and diagrams

- **Interpret and discuss data**
  - comparison of results with your original hypothesis
  - list of any factors which might have affected your results and how you could overcome these in future
  - a final conclusion

In small groups carry out an experiment to investigate one of the following.

1 Organise a class lottery. Get each person to choose 10 numbers, from 1 to 20. Have 10 separate draws and record who has a winning number each time (there may be more than one winner for each draw). Compare the theoretical and experimental probabilities of each player winning.

2 Investigate whether a drawing pin will land point up more often than point down. Use different-sized drawing pins to test whether the results are always the same.

3 Ask a member of your group to put ten coloured cubes in a bag, so that the rest of the group do not know what the colours are. Investigate how many times you need to pick a cube out and replace it in order to be able to predict accurately the contents of the bag.

4 Some people are luckier than others when rolling a dice.

5 A playing card usually lands face-up when dropped.

Extension Work

Choose one of the following tasks.

1 Working individually, write a report of your experiment using the checklist. Look again at the limitations of your experiment and think how you could overcome these, for example by increasing your sample size or choosing your sample using a different method.

2 In your small group, create a display which can be used as part of a presentation to show the other groups in your class how you carried out your experiment and what results you obtained. Look again at the limitations of your experiment and think how you could overcome these, for example by increasing your sample size or choosing your sample using a different method.

3 If you have completed your report, then consider a different problem from the list in **Exercise 15B**. Write a plan of how you would investigate it, including how to overcome any problems encountered in your first project.

This chapter is going to

○ Get you started on your GCSE course

BODMAS

You have already met BODMAS in Years 7 and 8. It gives the order in which mathematical operations are carried out in calculations.

Remember, that if a calculation is a string of additions and subtractions, or a string of multiplications and divisions, then the calculation is done from left to right.

B – Brackets

O – pOwers

DM – Division and Multiplication

AS – Addition and Subtraction

Example 16.1 ▷ Work out each of the following, using the order of operations given by BODMAS. Show each step of the calculation.

a $10 \div 2 + 3 \times 3$ **b** $10 \div (2 + 3) \times 3$

a Firstly, work out the division and multiplication, which gives $\quad 5 + 9$

Then work out the addition to give $\quad 14$

b Firstly, work out the bracket, which gives $\quad 10 \div 5 \times 3$

There is a choice between division and multiplication, so decide on the order by working from left to right:

Work out the left-hand operation first, which gives $\quad 2 \times 3$

Then work out the remaining operation to give $\quad 6$

Example 16.2 ▷ Work out: **a** $30 - 4 \times 2^2$ **b** $(30 - 4) \times 2^2$

Show each step of the calculation.

a Firstly, work out the power, which gives $\quad 30 - 4 \times 4$

Secondly, the multiplication, which gives $\quad 30 - 16$

Finally, the subtraction to give $\quad 14$

b Firstly, work out the bracket, which gives $\quad 26 \times 2^2$

Secondly, the power, which gives $\quad 26 \times 4$

Finally, the multiplication to give $\quad 104$

Exercise 16A

Do not use a calculator for this exercise.

1 Use BODMAS to work out each of the following.

   a $3 \times 6 + 7$ **b** $8 \div 4 + 8$ **c** $6 + 9 - 3$

   d $15 \div 3 + 7$ **e** $4 \times 6 \div 2$ **f** $3^2 \times 4 + 1$

2 Use BODMAS to work out each of the following. Remember to work out the brackets first.

   a $3 \times (3 + 7)$ **b** $12 \div (3 + 1)$ **c** $(9 + 4) - 4$

   d $4 \times (6 \div 2)$ **e** $20 \div (2 + 3)$ **f** $3 + (2 + 1)^2$

3 Write the operation that you do first in each of these calculations, and then work out each calculation.

   a $6 \times 2 - 3$ **b** $4 + 3 \times 5$ **c** $12 \div 2 - 3$

   d $15 - 5 \div 2$ **e** $6 \times 2 \div 1$ **f** $4 \times 6 - 3^2$

4 Use BODMAS to work out each of the following.

   a $16 - 4 \times 2$ **b** $7 \times (4 + 3)$ **c** $12 \div 4 + 8$

   d $(18 - 6) \div 4$ **e** $15 \div (4 + 1)$ **f** $12 + 4 \times 5$

   g $(24 \div 4) + 7$ **h** $5 + 3^2 \times 2$ **i** $5 \times 4 - 4^2$

   j $(3^2 + 1) \times 5$ **k** $4^2 \times (4 - 1)$ **l** $(6 - 1)^2 - 5$

5 Copy each of these calculations and then put in brackets to make each calculation true.

   a $4 \times 3 + 7 = 40$ **b** $10 \div 2 + 3 = 2$ **c** $18 \div 3 + 3 = 3$

   d $5 - 2 \times 4 = 12$ **e** $20 - 5 \times 2 = 30$ **f** $5 \times 12 - 8 = 20$

   g $10 - 2^2 \times 2 = 12$ **h** $10 - 2^2 \times 2 = 128$ **i** $24 \div 2^2 + 2 = 4$

6 Three dice are thrown. They give scores of 2, 4, and 5.

A class makes the following sums with the numbers. Work them out.

   a $(2 + 4) \times 5 =$ **b** $2 + 4 \times 5 =$ **c** $4^2 + 5 =$

   d $4 \times (5 - 2) =$ **e** $4 + 5 - 2 =$ **f** $(4 + 5)^2 =$

7 Three dice give scores of 2, 3 and 6. Copy each of the calculations below, putting $\times$, $+$, $\div$, $-$ or () in each calculation to make it true.

   a $6 \dots 2 \dots 3 = 12$ **b** $6 \dots 3 \dots 2 = 30$ **c** $3 \dots 6 \dots 2 = 16$

Adding and subtracting negative numbers

Negative numbers are used to describe many situations. For example, temperatures, distances above and below ground or how much money you have or haven't got in your bank account.

Example 16.3 ▷ John is £42.56 overdrawn at the bank. He gets his wages of £189.50 paid in and takes out £30 in cash. How much has he got in the bank now?

An overdrawn amount is negative, so the calculation is:

$$-42.56 + 189.50 - 30$$
$$= 189.50 - 72.56$$
$$= £116.94$$

Example 16.4 ▷ Find the missing number to make each of these calculations true.

a $10 + \boxed{} = 7$ **b** $-8 + \boxed{} = 12$ **c** $-9 - \boxed{} = 6$

You should be able to work out the answers to these using your knowledge of number facts. If you find this difficult, try visualising a number line, or for more difficult questions, rearrange the equation to find the unknown.

a $\boxed{} = 7 - 10 = -3$ **b** $\boxed{} = 12 + 8 = 20$

c $-\boxed{} = 6 + 9 = 15$, so $\boxed{} = -15$

Exercise 16B

1 The diagram shows a cliff, the sea and sea bed with various objects and places measured from sea level. Use the diagram to answer the questions below.

a How far above the sea bed are each of the following?
   i the submarine
   ii the lighthouse
   iii the plane

b How far below the lighthouse are each of the following?
   i the smugglers' cave
   ii the shark
   iii the submarine

c How far above (indicate with a +) or below (indicate with a –) the smugglers' cave are each of the following?
   i the plane
   ii the shark
   iii the submarine

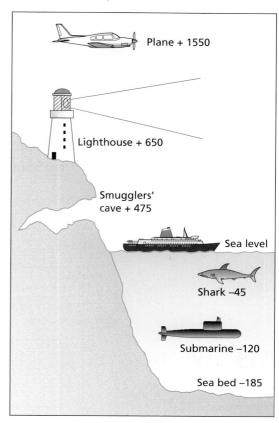

Plane + 1550

Lighthouse + 650

Smugglers' cave + 475

Sea level

Shark –45

Submarine –120

Sea bed –185

2 Copy and complete the balance column in the statement table below.

Transaction	Amount paid in	Amount paid out	Balance
			£64.37
Standing order		£53.20	£11.17
Cheque	£32.00		
Direct debit		£65.50	
Cash	£20.00		
Wages	£124.80		
Loan		£169.38	

3 Five temperatures are marked on the thermometer below.

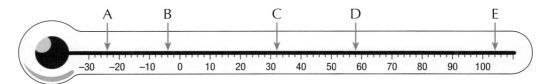

Calculate the difference between each of the following. Remember to give your answer in °C.

a A and B   **b** A and D   **c** A and E   **d** C and E

e B and E   **f** B and D   **g** A and C   **h** D and E

4 Copy and complete each of the following.

a If +£9 means a profit of nine pounds, then … means a loss of nine pounds.

b If +45 m means 45 metres above sea level, then … means 45 metres below sea level.

c If −15 minutes means 15 minutes before midday, then … means 15 minutes after midday.

d If a train moving forwards at 5 mph is represented by +5, then −5 represents ….

5 Calculate each of the following.

a 7 − 5 + 6   **b** 6 − 8 − 3   **c** −4 − 3 − 6   **d** −1 + 3 + 6

e 2 − (−5)   **f** −2 + (−3)   **g** −2 + (−4)   **h** +5 − (+7)

i −3 − −8 + 7   **j** +8 − + 8 + −2   **k** −6 + −6 + + 3   **l** −8 − −8 + − 1

m −9 − +2 − −1   **n** −45 + 89 − 27   **o** +7 − −6 + −1   **p** −6 − +5 + −5

6 Copy these number lines, filling in the missing numbers on each.

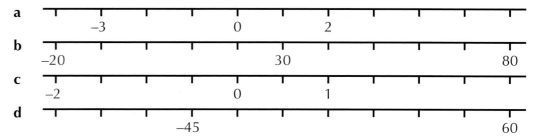

7 Work out the missing numbers from each of the boxes below in order to make each equation true.

a $3 + -5 = \boxed{}$ **b** $5 + \boxed{} = 9$ **c** $5 + \boxed{} = 2$

d $\boxed{} - -6 = 4$ **e** $-6 - \boxed{} = 3$ **f** $+ 7 - \boxed{} = 4$

g $-8 + -7 = \boxed{}$ **h** $\boxed{} - +4 = 0$ **i** $3 - 4 + \boxed{} = 6$

8 In a magic square, each row, column and diagonal adds up to the same 'magic number'. Copy and complete each of these magic squares and write down the 'magic number' for each one.

a

-3	-7	4
5		

b

-2		
	-4	-5
		-6

c

	-13	
-12	-5	-10

Multiples, factors and prime numbers

Example 16.5 Find the largest number less than 100 that is **a** a multiple of 3 **b** a multiple of 3 and 5

a This will be a number in the 3 times table that is close to 100:

$30 \times 3 = 90$

$31 \times 3 = 93$

$32 \times 3 = 96$

$33 \times 3 = 99$

$34 \times 3 = 102$

So, the largest multiple of 3 that is less that 100 is 99.

b Because 3 and 5 have no common factors, multiples common to 3 and 5 are multiples of 15:

15, 30, 45, 60, 75, 90, 105,…

So, the largest number under 100 that is a multiple of both 3 and 5 is 90.

Example 16.6 Find the factors of **a** 35 **b** 180

a Find all the products that make 35:

$1 \times 35 = 35$ $5 \times 7 = 35$

So, the factors of 35 are {1, 5, 7, 35}.

b $1 \times 180 = 180$ $2 \times 90 = 180$ $3 \times 60 = 180$ $4 \times 45 = 180$ $5 \times 36 = 180$

$6 \times 30 = 180$ $9 \times 20 = 180$ $10 \times 18 = 180$ $12 \times 15 = 180$

So, the factors are {1, 2, 3, 4, 5, 6, 9, 10, 12, 15, 18, 20, 30, 36, 45, 60, 90, 180}.

Remember that factors always come in pairs.

Do not use a calculator for this exercise.

1 Write down the first 5 multiples of each of the following.

   a   4   **b**   9   **c**   12   **d**   25

2 From the list of numbers below, write down those that are:

   a   multiples of 3   **b**   multiples of 5

   c   multiples of 4   **d**   multiples of 12

3	7	8	13	14	15	18	24
36	39	45	48	64	69	90	120

3 Find the largest number less than 50 that is:

   a   a multiple of 3   **b**   a multiple of 8

   c   a multiple of 7   **d**   a multiple of 6

4 Find the largest number less than 50 that is:

   a   a multiple of 3 and 4   **b**   a multiple of 5 and 9

   c   a multiple of 3 and 5   **d**   a multiple of 2 and 7

5 Write down all the factors of each number from 2 to 20.

6 **a**   Which of the numbers from 2 to 20 have only 2 factors? Use your answers to Question 5 to help you.

   b   What are these numbers called?

7 Write down all the factors of each of the following.

   a   48   **b**   52   **c**   60   **d**   75   **e**   100   **f**   130

8 Find the common factors of each of the following pairs of numbers.

   a   15 and 24   **b**   18 and 24   **c**   15 and 25   **d**   28 and 42

9 Copy the grid on the right.

Shade in, or cross out, the number 1.

Leave the number 2 blank and then shade in, or cross out, the rest of the multiples of 2.

Leave the number 3 blank and then shade in, or cross out, the rest of the multiples of 3. Some of them will have already been shaded in or crossed out.

Leave the number 5 blank and then shade in, or cross out, the rest of the multiples of 5. All but 3 of them will have already been shaded in or crossed out.

Leave the number 7 blank and then shade in, or cross out, the rest of the multiples of 7. All but 1 of them will have already been shaded in or crossed out.

The numbers that are left are the prime numbers up to 60.

1	2	3	4	5	6
7	8	9	10	11	12
13	14	15	16	17	18
19	20	21	22	23	24
25	26	27	28	29	30
31	32	33	34	35	36
37	38	39	40	41	42
43	44	45	46	47	48
49	50	51	52	53	54
55	56	57	58	59	60

Squares, square roots and powers

Example 16.7 ▷ Calculate **a** 22^2 **b** $\sqrt{289}$ **c** $\sqrt{600}$

    a You can either use the square button on your calculator or calculate 22×22.
        $22^2 = 22 \times 22 = 484$

    b Using the square root button on your calculator, $\sqrt{289} = 17$.

    c Using the square root button on your calculator, $\sqrt{600} = 24.5$ (rounded to 1 decimal place).

Example 16.8 ▷ Calculate 7^4.

    Using the power button on your calculator, $7^4 = 2401$.
    Remember $7^4 = 7 \times 7 \times 7 \times 7$.

Exercise 16D

Do not use a calculator for Questions 1 and 2.

1 Write down the value represented by each of the following.

    a 7^2 **b** 9^2 **c** 11^2 **d** 13^2 **e** 15^2

2 Write down the value represented by each of the following.

    a $\sqrt{36}$ **b** $\sqrt{64}$ **c** $\sqrt{100}$ **d** $\sqrt{144}$ **e** $\sqrt{196}$

You may use a calculator for Questions 3–6.

3 Find the value of the square of each of these numbers.

    a 19   **b** 24   **c** 25   **d** 32   **e** 53

4 Calculate each of the following. Round your answers to 2 decimal places.

    a $\sqrt{40}$ **b** $\sqrt{80}$ **c** $\sqrt{120}$ **d** $\sqrt{500}$ **e** $\sqrt{900}$

5 Calculate each of the following.

    a 4^5 **b** 12^3 **c** 13^4 **d** 21^3
    e 6^6 **f** 7^5 **g** 8^3 **h** 2^{12}

6 Work out the value of each of the following. What do you notice?

    a **i** $5^2 - 4^2$ **ii** 3^2
    b **i** $13^2 - 12^2$ **ii** 5^2
    c **i** $25^2 - 24^2$ **ii** 7^2
    d **i** $41^2 - 40^2$ **ii** 9^2

Do not use a calculator for the rest of this exercise.

7 $\sqrt{2} = 1.4142136$, $\sqrt{20} = 4.472136$, $\sqrt{200} = 14.142136$, $\sqrt{2000} = 44.72136$

Use this pattern to write down the value of each of the following.

a $\sqrt{20\,000}$ **b** $\sqrt{200\,000}$ **c** $\sqrt{2\,000\,000}$

8 Work out the value of each of the following.

a **i** 1^4 **ii** 1^8 **iii** 1^9

b **i** $(-1)^3$ **ii** $(-1)^4$ **iii** $(-1)^5$

9 Use your answers to Question 8 to work out the value represented by each of the following.

a 1^{23} **b** $(-1)^{10}$ **c** $(-1)^9$ **d** 1^{43}

Decimals in context: addition and subtraction

Think about where you may have seen decimal numbers recently.

The most obvious example of decimals in context is money. Prices in shops are usually given to 2 decimal places.

Speedometers in cars and weighing scales increasingly have digital displays involving decimal numbers and nutritional information on food packets, such as cereal, often involves decimal numbers too.

Nutritional Information per 100 g		
ENERGY	1600 kj	280 kcal
PROTEIN		4 g
CARBOHYDRATES		90 g
of which sugars		40 g
starch		50 g
FAT		0.7 g
of which saturates		0.2 g
FIBRE		0.9 g
SODIUM		0.45 g
VITAMINS:		(%RDA)
VITAMIN D µg	4.2	(85)
TIAMIN (B₁) mg	1.2	(85)
RIBOFLAVIN (B₂) mg	1.3	(85)
NIACIN mg	15.0	(85)

The next two lessons look at decimals in real life situations.

Example 16.9

Over the course of the year Mr Smith's gas bills were £125.23, £98.07, £68.45 and £102.67. What was the total cost of Mr Smith's gas for the year?

This is a straightforward addition problem:

```
  £125.23
  £ 98.07
  £ 68.45
+ £102.67
  £394.42
```

Example 16.10 ▷ Asif earns £2457.82 in a month. From this £324.78 is deducted for tax, £128.03 for National Insurance and £76.54 for other deductions. How much does Asif take home each month?

This is a subtraction problem. The easiest method to solve it, is to add up all the deductions and then subtract from his total pay.

Deductions

$$\begin{array}{r} \text{£324.78} \\ \text{£128.03} \\ + \text{£ 76.54} \\ \hline \text{£529.35} \end{array}$$

$$\begin{array}{r} ^{1\ 141\ 7}\text{£24}\cancel{5}7.\cancel{8}2 \\ - \text{£529.35} \\ \hline \text{£1928.47} \end{array}$$

---

1 Work out each of these.

a	1.8 + 6.9	**b**	6.63 + 7.2	**c**	9.05 + 5.92
d	7.5 − 2.9	**e**	5.67 − 1.87	**f**	7.83 + 1.26 − 7.48
g	9 − 3.7	**h**	12 + 2.36	**i**	8.02 − 1.27 − 2.34
j	12 − 3.47	**k**	8.07 − 2.68	**l**	15.32 − 4.1 − 2.03

2 A businesswoman pays 5 cheques into her bank account. The cheques are for £1456.08, £256.78, £1905.00, £46.89 and £694.58. How much did she pay in total?

3 Bert booked a holiday to Portugal over the Internet. His return flight cost £118 and his hotel accommodation cost £135.67 in Faro and £165.23 in Lisbon. He also spent £48.80 on train fares to travel between Faro and Lisbon. How much did his holiday cost him in total?

4 At the local shop Mary bought 2 tins of soup costing 57p each, a packet of sugar costing 78p, a loaf of bread costing £1.05, a packet of bacon costing £2.36 and a bottle of wine costing £4.23. What was her total bill?

5 Five books are placed on top of one another. The books are 2.3 cm, 15 mm, 3.95 cm, 1.75 cm and 18 mm thick. What is the total thickness of the pile of books in centimetres?

6 A cake was made using 132 grams of butter, 0.362 kilograms of flour and 96 grams of sugar. What is the total weight of these ingredients in kilograms.

7 Misha's bank account has £467.92 in it. She writes cheques for £67.50, £42.35 and £105.99. How much money will be left in Misha's account after these cheques have been cashed?

8 A new car has a list price of £6995.99. A delivery charge of £109.80 and a discount of £699.59 are taken off the list price. How much will a customer pay for the car?

9 A quadrilateral has a perimeter of 32 cm. The lengths of three of the sides are 8.23 cm, 3.48 cm and 12.96 cm. What is the length of the fourth side?

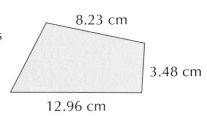

8.23 cm

3.48 cm

12.96 cm

10 William pays a standing order of £55 for fuel each month. Of this £55, £32.78 is for electricity, £12.61 is for gas and the rest is for heating oil. How much does William pay each month for heating oil?

11 Mr Brown's pay slip shows that he is paid a basic wage of £356.78 each week. In addition to his basic wage, he gets a bonus of £102.45. He has £67.82 tax, £34.80 National Insurance and £6.78 health insurance deducted from his pay. How much does Mr Brown take home each week?

Decimals in context: multiplication and division

Example 16.11 One chair costs £45.76 and a table costs £123.47. How much is a dining suite consisting of six chairs and a table?

This is a multiplication and addition problem:

Chairs cost		total cost	
	45.76		123.47
×	6	+	274.56
	274.56		398.03

Hence the total cost is £398.03.

Example 16.12 Eight litres of petrol and a can of oil together cost £8.95. If the can of oil costs £2.59, how much does one litre of petrol cost?

This is a subtraction and division problem:

Petrol costs
$$8.\overset{8\ 1}{\cancel{9}}5$$
$$-\ 2.59$$
$$6.36$$

$$\begin{array}{r} 0.795 \\ 8\overline{)6.3\overset{7\ 4}{6}0} \end{array}$$

Hence one litre of petrol costs 79.5 pence.

Exercise 16F

1 Work out

a	17.8	**b**	6.07	**c**	76.32	**d**	18.95
×	6	×	12	×	25	×	54

2 A packet of four AA batteries costs £4.15. How much money would you need to buy 9 packets of four AA batteries?

3 John bought 5 tins of cocoa costing £1.12 each and 7 jars of coffee costing £2.09 each. What was his total bill?

4 To make some shelves Mr George orders 7 pieces of wood 53.4 cm in length and 2 pieces of wood 178.5 cm in length. What is the total length of wood ordered by Mr George?

5 A crystal decanter costs £56.32 and a crystal wine glass costs £11.58. How much will a decanter and a set of six wine glasses cost?

6 Calculate each of the following.

   a   68.4 ÷ 6   **b**   8.36 ÷ 8   **c**   27.5 ÷ 11   **d**   32.5 ÷ 26

7 A table and four chairs are advertised for £385. If the table costs £106, how much does each chair cost?

You may use a calculator for the last three questions.

8 The distance from London to Leeds by train is 317.5 km. If a train takes 2 hours and 30 minutes to cover this distance, what is its average speed?

9 A man earns £27 746.40 a year. How much does he earn each month?

10 A holiday for 2 adults and 3 children costs £967.80 in total. If the cost per child is £158.20, what is the cost for each adult?

Long multiplication

You have already met several ways of doing long multiplication. Two of these are shown in the examples below. You may use any method you are happy with for Exercise 16G.

Example 16.13 Work out 164 × 56.

This multiplication could be done using the box method, as shown below.

×	100	60	4
50	5000	3000	200
6	600	360	24

```
   5000
   3000
    200
    600
    360
+    24
   9184
```

Example 16.14 Work out 238 × 76.

This multiplication could be done using the standard column method, as shown on the right.

```
     238
   ×  76
    1428
      2 4
   16660
      2 5
   18088
       1
```

Use any method you are happy with for the following questions and show all your working.

Check your answers with a calculator afterwards.

1 Work out each of the following. Remember to show your working.

   a 157×24 **b** 324×33 **c** 513×32 **d** 189×23

2 Work out each of the following.

   a 258×34 **b** 276×47 **c** 139×62 **d** 126×39

3 Work out each of the following.

   a 637×28 **b** 377×44 **c** 265×75 **d** 753×63

4 Work out each of the following.

   a 207×14 **b** 620×26 **c** 805×63 **d** 199×99

Long division

You should remember meeting two different ways of doing long division. These are shown below. You may use any method you are happy with to answer the Exercise 16H questions.

Example 16.15

Work out $858 \div 22$.

This division could be done using the standard column method, as below.

Step 1: Start by asking how many 22s there are in 8. There are none of course. So, include the next digit, which is 5, and ask how many 22s there are in 85. Working up the 22 times table (22, 44, 66, 88), we can see that there are 3. Write the 3 above the 5.

Step 2: Work out the value of 3×22 (= 66) and write it underneath 85. Then subtract 66 from 85 to find the remainder of 19.

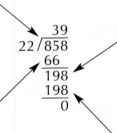

Step 3: Bring down the 8, next to the 19, to give 198.

Step 4: Now ask how many 22s there are in 198. Once again work up the 22 times table: 22, 44, 66, 88, 110, 132, 154, 176, 198. So there are exactly nine 22s in 198. Write the 9 above the 8.

As there is no remainder we can stop. The answer is 39.

Example 16.16 ▷ Work out $938 \div 36$.

This division has been done below, using repeated subtraction or 'chunking'.

$$
\begin{array}{r}
938 \\
-\underline{720} \quad (20 \times 36) \\
218 \\
-\underline{180} \quad (5 \times 36) \\
38 \\
-\underline{36} \quad (1 \times 36) \\
2
\end{array}
$$

As the remainder is less than 36 we can stop.

We have subtracted 36 a total of $20 + 5 + 1 = 26$ times, so the answer is 26 rem 2.

Exercise 16H

Use any method you are happy with for the following questions and show your working. Check your answers with a calculator afterwards.

1 Work out each of the following. These divisions have exact answers with no remainders. Remember to show your working.

    a $644 \div 23$ **b** $1224 \div 34$

    c $522 \div 18$ **d** $868 \div 28$

2 Work out each of the following. These divisions have exact answers with no remainders.

    a $840 \div 24$ **b** $2021 \div 47$

    c $532 \div 38$ **d** $741 \div 39$

3 Work out each of the following. These divisions will give remainders.

    a $637 \div 28$ **b** $877 \div 41$

    c $865 \div 25$ **d** $658 \div 33$

4 Work out each of the following. These divisions will give remainders.

    a $407 \div 14$ **b** $820 \div 16$

    c $915 \div 39$ **d** $799 \div 29$

Long multiplication and division in real-life problems

Example 16.17

Mr Winston buys a car for £36 480. He agrees to pay for it in 24 equal, monthly instalments. How much does he pay each month?

First you need to identify that this is a division problem, then choose which method to use.

The calculation is done below using the repeated subtraction method. We can ignore the zero on the end of £36 480, as long as we multiply the final answer by 10.

The 24 times table has been written out on the right to help.

$$
\begin{array}{rl}
3648 & \\
-\ 2400 & (100 \times 24) \\
\hline
1248 & \\
-\ 1200 & (50 \times 24) \\
\hline
48 & \\
-\ \ \ 48 & (2 \times 24) \quad + \\
\hline
0 & (152 \times 24)
\end{array}
$$

$1 \times 24 = 24$
$2 \times 24 = 48$
$5 \times 24 = 120$
$10 \times 24 = 240$
$20 \times 24 = 480$
$100 \times 24 = 2400$
$50 \times 24 = 1200$

Don't forget that we divided the starting number by 10, so the answer is £1520 per month.

Example 16.18

On checking his running diary, Paul finds that he has run an average of 65 miles a week during the last year. How many miles did he run in the year altogether?

You need to identify that this is a multiplication problem, recall that there are 52 weeks in a year, and then decide which method you are going to use.

The multiplication has been done below using the box method.

×	60	5
50	3000	250
2	120	10

So Paul has run a total of 3000 + 250 + 120 + 10 = 3380 miles.

Exercise 16I

Work out each of the following, showing your working.

Check your answers with a calculator afterwards.

1 A typist can type 54 words per minute on average. How many words can he type in 15 minutes?

2 Small chocolate eggs cost 43p each. Mrs Owen wants to buy an egg for each of her class of 28 students. How much will this cost her?

3 There are 972 students in a school. Each tutor group has 27 students in it. How many tutor groups are there?

4 In a road-race, there were 2200 entrants.

  a To get them to the start the organisers used a fleet of 52-seater buses. How many buses were needed?

  b The race was 15 miles long and all the entrants completed the course. How many miles in total did all the runners cover?

5 At a school fair, cups of tea were 32p each. The school sold 182 cups.

  a How much money did they take?

  b The school used plastic cups which came in packs of 25. They bought 24 packs. How many cups were left over?

6 **a** A cinema has 37 rows of seats. Each row contains 22 seats. How many people can sit in the cinema altogether?

  b Tuesday is 'all seats one price' night. There were 220 customers who paid a total of £572. What was the cost of one seat?

7 A library gets 700 books to distribute equally among 12 local schools.

  a How many books will each school get?

  b The library keeps any books left over. How many books is this?

8 The label on the side of a 1.5 kilogram cereal box says that there are 66 grams of carbohydrate in a 100g portion. How many grams of carbohydrate will Dan consume if he eats the whole box at once?

9 A first-class stamp costs 28p and a second-class stamp costs 19p. How much does it cost to send 63 letters first class and 78 letters second class?

10 Twelve members of a running club hire a minivan to do the Three Peaks race (climbing the highest mountains in England, Scotland and Wales). The van costs £25 per day plus 12p per mile. The van uses a litre of petrol for every 6 miles travelled. Petrol costs 78p per litre. The van is hired for 3 days and the total mileage covered is 1500.

  a How much does it cost to hire the van?

  b How many litres of petrol are used?

  c If the total cost is shared equally how much does each member pay?

GCSE past-paper questions

Questions 1–3 are from calculator-allowed papers

1 $17 \times \boxed{?} = 221$

What is the missing number?

AQA (SEG), Question 2, Paper 6, June 2001

2 A ribbon is 400 cm long.

    a How many pieces, each 36 cm long, can be cut from the ribbon?

    b What length, in centimetres, is left over?

AQA (NEAB), Question 7, Paper 2, June 2002

3 Here is a set of numbers

       3, 5, 6, 9, 15, 21

    a Which two of these numbers have a product of 15?

    b Which two of these numbers have a difference of 6 **and** a sum of 12?

    c Which of these numbers are prime?

    d Which of these numbers is a multiple of both 3 and 7?

EDEXCEL , Question 7, Paper 1, June 2001

4 Work out

    i $5 + (-2)$ **ii** $-3 - (-5)$ **iii** $-4 - 7$

AQA (NEAB), Question 7, Paper 2, June 2001

5 **a** A cinema has two screens.

       Screen One has 258 seats.   Screen Two has 126 seats.

       i Find the total number of seats.

       ii Screen One has 258 seats.

          One evening only 75 of them were used. How many seats in Screen One were **not** used?

    b At the cinema ice-creams cost 85p each. William buys 3 ice-creams. How much change does he get from £5?

AQA (SEG), Question 5, Paper 7, June 2001

6 Work these out

   a 52×9 **b** $328 \div 8$ **c** $5^2 \times 2^3$ **d** 127×23

OCR, Question 8, Paper 1, June 2001

7 Here is a number pattern.

   Line 1:   1   = 1
   Line 2:   1 + 3   = 4
   Line 3:   1 + 3 + 5   = 9
   Line 4:   1 + 3 + 5 + 7 = 16
   Line 5:   ……………   = …

   a Complete line 5.

   b What is the special name given to the numbers in the sequence 1, 4, 9, 16, …?

   c Line 3 adds up to 9. What does line 8 add up to?

   d Which line adds up to 100?

AQA (NEAB), Question 6, Paper 1, May 2002

8 **a** Use the calculation **12 × 18 = 216** to complete the two boxes.

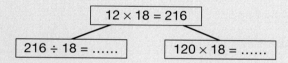

   b Use the calculation **24 × 26 = 624** to complete the three boxes.

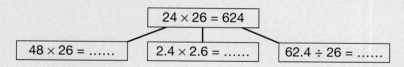

AQA (NEAB), Question 8, Paper 1, June 2001

9 The price of a box of chocolates is £4.32.

   There are 24 chocolates in the box.

   a Work out the cost of **one** chocolate.

   b Work out the total amount George should pay for the two boxes of chocolates.

   18 of the chocolates in the box are milk chocolates.

   c Work out 18 as a percentage of 24.

SPECIAL OFFER
Buy one box of chocolates
for £4.32
Buy a second box of
chocolates for half price

EDEXCEL, Question 14, Paper 3, June 2001

10 Here is a flow diagram.

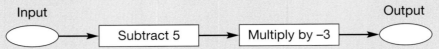

a What is the output when the input is 3?

b What is the input when the output is –21?

AQA (NEAB), Question 9, Paper 1, Nov 2001

11 a i Work out 2^3.

  ii Work out $(-2) \times (-3)$.

b A sequence begins: 2, 1, ...

The rule for continuing the sequence is

  MULTIPLY THE LAST NUMBER BY 2 AND SUBTRACT 3

Write down the next two numbers in the sequence.

AQA (SEG), Question 2, Paper 7, June 2001

12 Colin buys two cups of tea and three cups of coffee.

He pays £4.65 altogether.

The price of a cup of tea is 84 pence.

What is the price of a cup of coffee?

AQA (SEG), Question 3, Paper 7, June 2001

Published by HarperCollins*Publishers* Limited
77–85 Fulham Palace Road
Hammersmith, London W6 8JB

Browse the complete Collins catalogue at
www.collinseducation.com

© HarperCollins*Publishers* Ltd 2003
10 9 8 7 6 5
ISBN-13 978 0 00 713860 9
ISBN-10 0 00 713860 1

British Library Cataloguing in Publication Data
A Catalogue record for this publication is available from the
British Library

Edited by John Day
Design and typesetting by Jordan Publishing Design
Project Management by Nicola Tidman
Covers by Tim Byrne
Illustrations by Nigel Jordan, Tony Wilkins and Barking Dog Art
Proofreading by Amanda Whyte and Jenny Wong
Production by Sarah Robinson
Printed and bound by Printing Express, Hong Kong

The publishers would like to thank the many teachers and advisers
whose feedback helped to shape *Maths Frameworking*.

The publishers thank the Qualifications and Curriculum Authority
for granting permission to reproduce questions from past SAT
papers for Key Stage 3.

AQA (NEAB)/(SEG) examination questions are reproduced by
permission of the Assessment and Qualifications Alliance.

The publishers thank London Qualifications Ltd for granting
permission to reproduce questions from past Edexcel GCSE papers.

OCR examination questions are reproduced with the kind
permission of OCR.

Every effort has been made to trace copyright holders and to obtain
their permission for the use of copyright material. The author and
publishers will gladly receive any information enabling them to
rectify any error or omission in subsequent editions.

You might also like to visit:
www.harpercollins.co.uk
The book lover's website